LIKE
NESS

LIKE NESS

DAVID MACFARLANE

fathers, sons,
a portrait

DOUBLEDAY CANADA

Doubleday Canada and colophon are registered trademarks
of Penguin Random House Canada Limited.

LIBRARY AND ARCHIVES CANADA CATALOGUING IN PUBLICATION
Title: Likeness / David Macfarlane.
Names: Macfarlane, David, 1952- author.
Identifiers: Canadiana (print) 20200212575 | Canadiana (ebook) 20200212583 |
ISBN 9780385693714 (hardcover) | ISBN 9780385693721 (EPUB)
Subjects: LCSH: Macfarlane, David, 1952-—Family. | LCSH: Macfarlane, Blake. |
LCSH: Parents of terminally ill children—Biography. | LCSH: Cancer—
Patients—Biography. | LCSH: Fathers and sons—Biography. |
LCSH: Bereavement. | LCGFT: Biographies.
Classification: LCC RC265.6.M33 M33 2020 | DDC 362.19699/40092—dc23

Cover and book design: Kate Sinclair

Printed and bound in Canada

Published in Canada by Doubleday Canada, a division of
Penguin Random House Canada Limited

www.penguinrandomhouse.ca

10 9 8 7 6 5 4 3 2 1

Penguin
Random House
DOUBLEDAY CANADA

To Gillian and Ron. And to Effy.

Much of what I do in creating a painting is construct it to engage the viewer. However, I understand that every viewer will enter into the imaginative space of the painting in a particular way. I don't expect to have any control over this.

John Hartman

Between 2014 and 2020, John Hartman completed the portraits of forty Canadian writers. *David Macfarlane above Hamilton* (oil on linen, 60" x 66") can be viewed at manylives.art.

one

Begin outside. That's where all the grey is. Start at the back. That's where the mists of time are.

There is a small rectangle there. It's to the right of my right eye. Not to my actual eye. It's to the right of my right eye in a painting of me. I can show you. You can see what I mean.

Get closer, and if you squint a little you can imagine a concrete playground. Girls' Side. Boys' Side. No colour because there wasn't much.

Earl Kitchener Junior Public School was erected on Dundurn Street, in the city of Hamilton, in the province of Ontario, in 1914.

Erected. Har-dee-har.

"Slang."

Dun coats. Dun air. The back stairs, clang, clang, clang, clang.

"Incomplete sentences." Mr. Parsons' irritated red cursive.

Children shout in the dull air. The volume at recess is remarkable. And under the stairs, clang, clang, clang, a boy (slight, dark-haired, doomed) is telling a joke to the huddle of fall jackets around him.

You cut off his arms.

He's reciting the joke, actually—as if it's a lyric to a tune he isn't singing.

2

When John Hartman, who is an artist I know, asked me if I'd give him a tour of Hamilton, I said that it would be a pleasure just like my father used to say: it would be a pleasure. Not that my father said it would be a pleasure that often. My father didn't say anything that often.

My father grew up in a red brick house, not far from the red brick house in which I grew up. I could explain their approximate geography with the oil painting of Hamilton that Hartman finished a few months after I gave him my guided tour.

Even though the streets in Hartman's composition are suggested as much as they are drawn, I could use the picture to point to where my father's childhood home used to be and (about the length of a Winsor & Newton paintbrush away) the playground of Earl Kitchener Junior Public School. They were that close.

3

I read those two passages—the part about the playground and the part about where my father's old house used to be—to my son, Blake, when he was in the hospital. I wasn't sure what he thought of them. This wasn't unusual.

Blake was terrible at pretending to be interested in something he wasn't interested in. This was partly because when he really was interested he couldn't help looking really, really interested. If he was listening to a story that he wanted to hear he'd have exactly the expression you'd want on the face of someone to whom you are telling a story.

This had been true of him all his life. He withered in the face of boredom and, as a result, he learned at an early age to avoid it when he could. Once, when we were walking home from kindergarten or nursery school or swimming lessons or somewhere and we passed Trinity-St. Paul's, at the corner of Robert and Bloor Streets in Toronto, I asked the six-year-old Blake if he had any interest in going to church. "Nope," he said.

I remember this clearly—in part because his lack of hesitation made me laugh but also because walking home from kindergarten or swimming lessons or whatever it was on this particular occasion is the walking-home that I think of when I wonder, as I sometimes do, when we last held hands when we walked anywhere.

I looked down at him. I wasn't pressing the issue. I had no evangelical intent. I was just interested in the prompt confidence of his answer.

"Why not?" I asked.

"I'm not a religious guy."

Blake thought playing with his *Star Wars* figurines on Sunday mornings was a better use of his time. He might have been right.

By the time he was a teenager, Blake composed electronic music. He made beats. He edited documentaries. He directed music videos. He worked as a DJ. He had an animation camera set up in his bedroom. He kept journals. He drew a lot. He watched lots of movies I'd never seen and listened to lots of music I'd never heard of.

He liked to work. He could sit at his computer, headphones on, for hours.

He usually had a few things on the go. Even when he was sick, he was doing some editing when he could. He was always working on a song. He was taking piano lessons. He played guitar and, when he did, he seemed to find his way to melodies that sounded more like East Africa than the standard three chords of the blues progressions I played. He was building a climbing wall in his bedroom so he could practise rock climbing when he had more use of his arms. He was making a *Millennium Falcon* out of Lego. Because it was fun. Because it reminded him of Sunday mornings playing with his *Star Wars* figurines.

It was difficult for Blake to entertain long-term projects when he was sick. His collaborations waxed and waned with his energies and with the cycles of treatment and medication. This made him sad.

There was something, though, that he had in mind. He spoke to me about it now and then. He wasn't yet sure what it would be, exactly. He could see it as a graphic novel. Maybe animation.

His friends. Our friends. His colleagues. Our family. A small, stalwart community had rallied around Blake's illness, and Blake had been fretting for a while about how to thank them. He tried writing a group letter. I remember he asked me to look at drafts a couple of times. But there was something about this that he found wearisome. It began to feel like a task. That's when he came up with the graphic novel idea. Perhaps an animated short.

It would be the history of his illness—a story that he would tell in a very Blake kind of way. It started as a doodle—a comic-like sketch about getting his medical marijuana card. But he refined it a bit, and as he did it occurred to him that this was a way for him to tell a bigger story: what it was like to be not-sick and then so sick.

Three panels, in black pen and filled-in with Sharpie. And somehow, in the shuffle of everything, I still have that piece of paper. I remember being struck with the composition: distant, closer, close up. The simple lines do actually look like Blake.

It would be quirky, and dark, and funny. It would be something he could work on whether in the hospital or at home, and when it was done he could send it online as his thank-you. To friends. To family. To a few doctors and a lot of nurses.

I thought this was a good idea. I could see it would engage him.

I asked about it occasionally, but I didn't want to appear like I was pushing. I'd long ago learned that creative projects, much like girlfriends, were subjects Blake would address without much in the way of input from his father.

The story of his illness was something he found difficult to tell— and not because the subject of an unexpected illness was emotion- ally overwhelming, although sometimes it was. What Blake found difficult was describing what being sick was like—how it made everything different, and how everything stayed different, even in remission. Perhaps especially in remission. Blake said he felt like he was in another universe sometimes.

Blake watched a lot of movies when he was sick. An awful lot. When I arrived in one of the many hospital rooms he was in, he was usually watching something on his computer, propped open on his bed-tray. When he was at home, living in the apartment we have in our basement, he was often on his couch, under a blanket and surrounded by carefully positioned pillows, watching (I some- times joked, but it wasn't far wrong) every single movie that had ever been made.

He was catholic in his enthusiasms. He'd seen *El Topo*, and *Vertigo* and *Day for Night* and *Rashomon*. But he'd also been through all of *Star Trek* and *Star Wars*. Several times. It was hard to come up with a horror movie—whether fantastically bad or very good—that he hadn't seen. He knew his Dario Argento but he also knew his

Vincent Price. We both loved *The Shining*. He was a big fan of the Mexican director Guillermo del Toro.

This is only an approximate guide to Blake. But approximations are all we've got to go on. Even the most thoughtful and painstaking portraits are educated guesses. And so, when I try to imagine what Blake had in mind as the thank-you gift for the people who were helping him get better, I'm probably only getting it partly right. Quite possibly I'm getting it entirely wrong. I can picture his delighted, engaged expression and I can bring to mind his blank, baleful stare. Either is possible. And that's the problem. This is the best I can do.

But there's one thing I'm sure of. There would have to be something a little off-kilter, a little unusual about how Blake would recount the history of his illness. That's a given. And I think his friends and family would agree. It would be the history of an illness, but with something like a horror movie mixed in. It would be the history of an illness, but recounted during a time when a dark force is gaining control of a hospital. Or something like that.

Blake's history of his illness would be a little quirky, for sure. A little unconventional. My guess: a narrator who inexplicably pops up every now and then to speak directly to camera or, in the case of a graphic novel, directly from the frame of a drawing.

This, in itself, wouldn't be so strange. Specialists appear in hospitals. They say things. Then they disappear. And a nurse who specializes in palliative care is hardly a fantastic element in a cancer hospital. What would be strange (especially in the bright, white busy-ness of that hospital light) is this narrator's calm, unhurried dignity.

She carries herself like a retired dancer—which adds to her mystery. I'd guess her age at about fifty. But even though her back and shoulders and neck are proudly unbowed, there is the direct acknowledgement of grief in her bearing. She is a mother, too.

This is apparent. This is part of who she is. That she is a mother is part of her empathy. She understands what she is witnessing. She knows the great, terrible weight of it. She does not pretend it is other than what it is. And this is why a visual medium (an animated short, a graphic novel) is so enviably direct. You don't have to say all this.

She seemed to just appear in Blake's room—on that New Year's Day. We'd never seen her before. We never saw her again. She was (you could sense immediately) kind. She was Indian, I think. She was friendly, even a little funny as I recall, but there was something so unhurried about her she seemed to have come from a different dimension of hospital life.

That's why she would make such a good narrator. She is the sort of presence who can show up from time to time in a story and tell you, face to face, what's going on.

The various departments of Blake's interests and projects and jobs had been sequestered into different corners of the various communal apartments he'd lived in as a university student (Film Studies, mostly) and then, as a graduate of Film Studies mostly, as a young guy starting out and trying to earn a living in Toronto—a sometimes editor, producer, cameraman, DJ, director, composer. He liked living downtown. He'd go out dancing with friends to places I'd never heard of.

Effy Min was his close companion, kindred spirit, confidante . . . And when I e-mailed Effy to ask about the music Blake was listening to at university, she answered: "During Flying Lotus phase (4th year) we were obsessed with Actress, Teebs, Shlomo—this being when Blake spent every single weekend evening making beats & led to what was imo his best work."

Parents are not wrong to think their children speak another dialect. The rhythms and jokes are different. So are the points of reference. But when Effy answered my e-mail I felt particularly (as my mother used to describe the condition) clueless.

4

My father's stories of Hamilton were brief, congenial outbursts of information. His idiosyncratic history seemed all the more idiosyncratic because the house that contained this history—the house in which he'd grown up—no longer existed. The solid, dignified red brick residence (with its veranda and wisteria) was known by everyone who spoke of it (my mother, mostly) simply as "Duke Street." It was at the corner of MacNab, one block west of James. Duke Street was torn down in the 1970s.

It would have been quite different had my father grown up somewhere far away, in a place rarely visited. But we were basically from the same part of Hamilton. His childhood memories were geographically centred on what I considered the outer edge of the neighbourhood in which I lived. I sometimes walked past Duke Street on my way to swim class at the YMCA.

The locations of my father's childhood and my childhood were practically identical. But this was not obvious when I was growing up. His Hamilton seemed to exist in another world.

In his Hamilton there was the aunt who fell from a minstrel gallery while dancing on a railing at a New Year's Eve party. "In the twenties," my father said, by way of explanation. He couldn't have been old enough to witness the accident, but my father's description of the moment before the tragedy was as spare as a James Thurber cartoon. Men in dinner jackets looking up. A pretty young woman in a fringed silk dress and high spirits, looking down. My father's story depended on little more than the slightly ironic emphasis he put on the words "minstrel" and "gallery"—as if a frivolity of residential architecture was bound to end badly. She broke her back, and for decades thereafter was carried to family gatherings on a pallet of pillows and Afghan rugs.

And there was my father's uncle. He was a doctor. My father would whisper: "A dipsomaniac." My father's erratic uncle had trained in Vienna and was a well-known specialist in venereal diseases. Hamilton's proximity to the American border meant that he was occasionally blindfolded, driven to a farmhouse somewhere in the vicinity of Niagara Falls, and called upon to treat famous mobsters for the clap. Apparently the pay for this was quite good.

5

I didn't know much about the music Blake liked, but I knew enough to understand that music was a thread. He was a pretty good drummer and he played around on piano and guitar. But he didn't call himself a musician—not in the way musicians call themselves musicians. He was, however, musical—a lot more musical than I am. He was a teenager when I realized that he had the capacity to dream up a melody. Out of the blue. I'd have been only slightly more astonished had he revealed to me that he could fly.

His music was strange, often eerie. But there was a pop happiness to it. Blake's love of dancing was never far away from what he was composing.

After he got sick there were vocals he recorded that were more keening than singing. But there was something in them that made you curious about what was going to happen next.

There was music in his editing. And there was music in the way, when he was doing camera, he'd come in close on a pair of hands and stay there, for what would prove to be a long and revealing time. This wasn't only rhythm—although Blake's sense of rhythm, like the inventiveness of his beats, was sharp. It was more a matter of wanting things (like movies, like stories) to unfold with the same balance of surprise and inevitability as music.

What made Blake's career path a little confusing (to my mother, for one) was a concept that seemed to cause no confusion for Blake. He wasn't going to be any one thing—at least, not for a while. He wasn't going to stop being a documentary film editor, for instance, because he was going to be a music video director. Being a music producer didn't cancel out being a cameraman. And being a DJ was not unrelated to composing electronic music, and composing electronic music was not unrelated to creating an animated short and the process of animation wasn't so removed from writing a graphic novel. And so on.

"Ours was a simpler age," my mother would say when I tried to explain to her what Blake was doing.

My parents must have felt some of the same anxiety when I announced to them my first not-entirely-ludicrous career ambition: I was going to be a sportswriter for the *Hamilton Spectator*. This was not a goal I ever achieved, but for a few years it was my standard answer to anyone (adults, inevitably) who asked what I was going to do when I grew up. How somebody became a sportswriter for the *Hamilton Spectator* must have been as obscure a path to my parents as Blake's ambition to become a film director was to me. But Blake's game was far more complex than mine ever was. The future he pictured was in an emerging, not-yet-formed, still-on-the-drawing-board world. This was not at all how my future looked when I was in my twenties. When I was starting out, any magazine or newspaper I could work for was one that my parents, maybe even my grandparents, would have at least heard of.

I think it's fair to say that the broad outline of Blake's view of his future would be something like this: if civilization was going to survive environmental, economic, and democratic cataclysm (not an outcome on which he'd be willing to bet) everything was going to be different. Very different. As I pointed out to my mother, if your general context is the collapse theory, career planning can be complicated. Certainly, more complicated than her generation, or mine, had known career planning to be. "Sometimes," she'd say at a conversational impasse such as this, "I don't think I can get out of this world fast enough."

A combination of all the things Blake did was what Blake was becoming. I couldn't know what that would be. Not knowing was always, for me, part of who he was—but not as big a part as you might think. I don't ever remember worrying about Blake. From the time he was a little boy there was a core of confidence to him that seemed mostly unshaken by a few less-than-brilliant marks and some unimpressed teachers. He excelled at what he wanted to excel at. There was something out there—some mash-up of all those sequestered corners of all those grotty apartments. And whatever it was, it was bound to be obscure to anyone with one foot in the analog world. To be absolutely specific, it was bound to be obscure to the subject of John Hartman's painting.

The portrait measures five feet by five and a half feet, painted on a stretched, unframed rectangle. Oil on Belgian linen.

The composition is that of an enormous passport photo. As is true for owners of passports, the painting can be identified with a few basic points of information.

Surname: Macfarlane. Given Names: David Blakely. Date of Birth: 19 Aug 52.

Hair: long, grey and thin. Eyes: more grey than blue, more sad than happy, and, in their actual measurement in the painting, as big as oyster shells. Attire: open-necked white shirt with blue and red stripes that my wife gave me for my birthday a few years ago. Place of Birth: in the background.

Were you to come upon this painting by surprise, with no context whatsoever, you would notice a few things about it. Hartman's elevated point of view, for one. This is characteristic. Looking at his paintings can feel like you are approaching a city for a landing. The writer Noah Richler evoked the image of Icarus (wings; sun) in an essay on Hartman's work, and it's true: there is something dizzying about the perspective. There is something dangerous but irresistible in the silence (only the wind rushing) of that height. We are gliding over Hamilton, the noise of urban life far below. Hartman says he dreamed of flying as a child.

You would also note a certain affluence. A certain privilege. A certain whiteness. The subject's age might suggest that this is not a picture of a man with an entirely firm grasp of the contemporary. The ground has shifted underneath feet that are not visible in the painting.

But the zigs and zags of Blake's professional career did have one underlying principle that I understood. It had been a factor in his general storytelling technique from the time of his grade-school compositions: nothing could be boring.

This didn't mean that a story had to be spectacular—although Blake had nothing against the spectacular. *Mad Max: Fury Road*, for example. Thumbs up. (This was the expression we used to sign off in e-mails when he was in the hospital. No emoji. We'd just type: *thumbs up*.) But a story could be quiet. It could be funny. It could be gentle. It could be sad.

It just couldn't be boring.

He wasn't in favour of narrative floundering around. The playground, for instance. He raised the point in the hospital that day. Why start with the grey rectangle of the playground? To the right of my right eye.

These were the kinds of questions Blake asked when I read to him from what I was working on. What's with the playground? So I told him.

The painting is: my head and shoulders in the foreground; Hamilton in the background. Its elements are dashes of colour. Some of the brushstrokes are as small as the words on this page. Most are larger than that. But not by much.

The portrait is not very figurative when the strokes and swirls of oil paints are looked at closely—which is one of the things that's fun to do when you have a huge painting of yourself in your living room. When I let the overall effect of my grey hair and sad, oyster-size eyes slip into my peripheral vision and I focus on what I take to be the detail with which Hartman works, I wonder how he knows that these abstractions of colour will add up to something.

Language and music suggest an order. One word comes before a second word. This note follows that. What we normally understand as the sequential nature of time is as predictable as a golf course. The dogleg of the eighth always comes after the footbridge of the seventh. The putter follows the nine iron which follows the three which follows the driver.

Paintings are rarely sequential by nature. If golf games were paintings, all eighteen holes would be played simultaneously— because paintings show you everything about themselves at the same time.

This doesn't mean you *see* everything at the same time in a painting. Seeing a painting is another matter.

The dead must miss the world's light with the same pang of sadness by which we miss the dead. It must be a souvenir of our world that they wish they had. Wherever they are. And that's what makes the painter's art so complex. If you look closely at a small section of the painting in our living room, and think of it not as an effect of pigment but as the literal representation of an hour's work, the order in which the work was done is not apparent. Where do you start? Where do you begin when you are painting light?

That two follows one and three follows two are matters of statistical truth but not absolute. Or so Carl Jung suspected. Or so my friend told me on the night I first took LSD, which I mention now only because it happens to be germane to the painting. That's why Jung became interested in the ancient Chinese divination text the *I Ching*. Or so my friend told me when we sat on the lid of a culvert in the woods of the Niagara Escarpment that night. He had his doubts about causality. Jung, that is. It was exceptionally good LSD.

What I told Blake was that I wanted to begin with the playground because once, on a summer night long ago, I had ended up outside Earl Kitchener Junior Public School. It was the summer I worked at the steel company. We were out, roaming the neighbourhood. Roaming the neighbourhood in the middle of the night with friends while insanely high was one of the great delights of being a teenager, in Hamilton, in the late 1960s. Imo.

We were perfectly safe. Of this we were certain. We didn't think in these terms at all (and that, in itself, is evidence of how certain we were), but we were white, middle-class teenagers. We'd have had to throw a rock through a picture window before anyone would dream of calling the police. Even if we were on the swings in the playground at two in the morning. Even if we were (as must have been obvious to anybody peering at us from a bedroom window) on drugs. But nonetheless we tried to be quiet. It was our strong preference to have no encounters with other (particularly, adult) human beings.

The tumult of trees on our walk to Earl Kitchener was a culled version of the woods along the side of the escarpment. The leaves were up-lit in the same dramatic way trees are up-lit in contemporary horror movies. (See: *Get Out*. See: *It*. Both of which I did, with Blake, when he was sick, but not stuck in the hospital.) At night, the big, high boughs looked like billows of dense smoke.

The deciduous forest combined with street lights and hallucinogenic drugs to great effect. And what I told Blake was: I discovered that I could stand under the trees that bordered that concrete playground and name the names of schoolmates I hadn't thought of in years. In years! I could go up and down the rows of those varnished desks. Zintar! Ingrid! Howard! Karen! Gordon! Lonnie! Sian! Guntar! Linda! Terry! Cindy! John! Malka! I had no idea those memories were still there. Donny! Out of nowhere I remembered Donny! Franklin! I could remember Franklin. I could remember Donna! I could remember Susan's plaid hair ribbon and white sweater! I discovered I could name all my teachers—from kindergarten (Miss Thompson) to grade six (Mr. Parsons). I remembered where the honour rolls were in the long, polished hallways, and the gloomy Group of Seven reproductions, and the portrait of the Queen. The stairs at the back had a very particular clang. That grey playground was like a portal that led straight to what, until that psychedelic moment, were forgotten details of my past.

"It was quite amazing," I said to Blake.

He wasn't convinced. He sometimes pointed out things to me about writing. Things like: at the beginning of *Get Out*, when a young couple hit a deer on the road on their way for a weekend at the young woman's creepy parents' place, the moment the deer strikes the car is given the weight it's given (violent, terrifying) because hitting the deer has something to do with the rest of the movie.

Blake's observations would sometimes be followed by a pause.

Blake felt as most sons do at some point in their relationship with their fathers: obliged to state the obvious. Hitting a deer is not written into the script of *Get Out* only because the handsome black boyfriend and the beautiful white girlfriend can remember it happening. Just because something could be recalled didn't mean it was worth a detailed description.

Pause.

The closer you get to the painting, the harder it becomes to guess what follows what. You leave the narrative of a portrait, and end up someplace new. You are a musician following a melody not in the score. You are a golfer who, for eighteen holes, follows a different order than the sequence of strokes. "Life is not a series of gig lamps symmetrically arranged," Virginia Woolf once observed. "Life is a luminous halo, a semi-transparent envelope surrounding us from the beginning of consciousness to the end."

As a luminous, semi-transparent case in point, I mentioned to Blake that I was thinking of including something about a professor I once had. Dr. Nancy Lindheim was majestic in her black academic gown. Blake was skeptical.

"But listen," I said to him.

I'd just got back from refilling Blake's two (as stipulated by Blake) glasses with the correct ratio of ice and water and I was sitting in the orange vinyl chair at the end of his bed.

The fall after my summer job at the steel company in Hamilton I was a first-year student at the University of Toronto. That was the reason for the summer job. My favourite course was Introduction to Modern English Literature. Tuesday and Thursday. Second floor, Larkin Building. No prerequisites.

"You know *To the Lighthouse*?"

Blake nodded. Patiently.

"Well, there's a painter in *To the Lighthouse* . . ."

Her name is Lily Briscoe and with her brush raised, Lily stands on the Ramsay family's holiday beach on the Hebrides. The lighthouse that James, the young son of the Ramsays, hopes to visit the next day is on the horizon.

But in my memory of this scene, Professor Lindheim is always present. That's what I explained to Blake. I remember Professor Lindheim reading a paragraph from *To the Lighthouse* in response to a question somebody in the class had asked. And I remember being dazzled. Yes, actually: dazzled. My attention was held by the point under the seminar table where her black stockings met the hem of her academic gown. That was part of it, I will admit. But so was the fact that I'd never met anyone who knew as much about anything as Professor Lindheim knew about *To the Lighthouse*.

Professor Lindheim reaches for her well-worn copy. And as Lily Briscoe stands there, buffeted by the sea breeze and made anxious by the irritating Charles Tansley, Professor Lindheim reads.

Her paperback does not look like it will survive very many more terms. Her steady, respectful voice is further confirmation of what the first year of college is beginning to make clear: I don't know very much. I'd never known anybody as smart as Professor Lindheim.

With her brush raised, Lily Briscoe pauses. "For a moment it stayed trembling in a painful but exciting ecstasy in the air. Where to begin?"

6

I know a lot about Hartman's painting. I even know the houses that aren't in it anymore. I know characters long gone. In regards to this painting (and only this painting) I could be one of those threadbare tour guides encountered outside cathedrals. I'd hold my closed umbrella aloft amid the throngs. Who I was and how I came to be such an expert would be mysterious subtext to my one-hour, three-times-a-day-in-high-season walking tours. Was I a failed academic? A defrocked priest? Or was I someone who had, as a young traveller, fallen in love with this cathedral and decided, therefore, to devote my life to studying it? Who knew? But what would be clear to the small cluster of people who followed me from flying buttresses to crypt to rose window is that I know my subject very well.

Look, I could say. Here. I'd point exactly to an area of the Hartman painting behind where I was standing without turning around or taking my gaze away from my audience.

This is the part of Hamilton where my grandmother was born. It's well to the east of the downtown core, as you can see. She lived in a neighbourhood of understated respectability. Its generous-sized homes were built before the steel mills and their attendant industries dominated the east end.

Victorian. Also red brick. They were mostly rooming houses by the Second World War.

My father was a doctor. So was his father. They shared an office for a few years when my father was starting out. I could show you the Medical Arts Building. It's on James Street, although it's not actually visible in the painting. In the imaginary space of Hartman's painting James Street is behind my head—which is very visible. In fact, my head is central to the painting although (speaking as a viewer and not as a subject) I tend to be drawn to the background.

7

The Medical Arts Building was like the central fortress of the more sprawling fiefdom of Hamilton. That's how it looked to me when I played with friends in the woods on the side of the escarpment. There were not many bigger buildings in Hamilton when I was growing up.

The grid of the city was splayed below us, just as it is in Hartman's painting. Just as it was (so I told John Hartman on our walk through my old neighbourhood) when I first dropped acid. The elevated point of view feels uncannily accurate to me—as if Hartman has cut a deck to the very card I had in mind. But even from that height and from that distance you could see the corner windows of my father's office. He was an eye doctor. My grandfather was an ear, nose and throat man. Suite 610.

Sharing a practice was not a happy arrangement—at least according to my mother it wasn't. My grandfather underpaid his junior partner. That's what the wife of the junior partner thought. But even more damning than Pappy's stinginess was his emotional distance. These were opinions my mother expressed more than once.

Over time, my mother's critique of what she referred to simply as "Hamilton" got boiled down to a few repeated soliloquies—"Hamilton" being mostly, but not exclusively, that portion of the city's population to which she was related by marriage. And one of the most recurrent of her subjects was something my father never denied—although it seemed always to bother him a good deal less than it bothered her.

My father's father never invited my father to play golf. Not once. My mother could number the missed opportunities.

Not when my father was a teenager at Westdale Collegiate. Not when he was a medical student. Not when he was an intern. Not when he was a resident at the Mayo. And not when he was a young ophthalmologist, struggling to support his growing family on wages that a short-order cook would consider skint. My mother said.

My grandfather was sporty in the modest, let's-not-get-carried-away manner in which gentlemen were sporty in those days. He played a passable game of tennis. He went to a fishing lodge with the same group of men for a weekend or two every summer (bass; Georgian Bay.) He golfed.

He was the shortest in the ascending line of four generations of men with Blakely as their middle name. Toward the end of his life he took on the oval dignity best accommodated by a three-piece suit. But he had a strong, active centre of gravity right up to the end.

Let's put it this way. My mother said. Until his stroke Pappy could have picked up the telephone any day of the week and invited his son to the golf club. It wouldn't have killed him.

He may have simply run out of whatever sporty energy he had expended on his first three children. This happens. Or (and this was the explanation my mother favoured) he may have been less jovial, less recreational, less physical in his relationship with his youngest because a childhood brush with polio left my father's left leg thinner and weaker than the right. His limp was very slight—more a characteristic of his gait than an impairment. But it was there. And in her recaps of family history it was at this juncture that my mother usually paused. She never actually said that my father's illness cut him off from paternal warmth and affection. That's what the pause was for.

8

Princess Margaret Hospital is about a twenty-minute walk from our house in downtown Toronto. But Blake and I took the street-car on the day of his second round of tests because Blake felt (his word) crappy. It would be a few hours before they had the results. So Blake and I walked over to the Art Gallery of Ontario to pass the time. It's only four blocks away from the hospital.

We'd often gone to the AGO, the four of us, when Caroline and Blake were kids. And Blake may have suggested going mostly because, unlike the hospital, it was familiar. I don't remember. I don't think I saw a single thing we looked at.

Back at Princess Margaret, I sat beside Blake in the windowless bright light of the first of what would be many bright rooms and listened to what the oncologist told him.

We hugged for a long time when the doctor left. We were both crying. I remember noticing that his hair smelled just as it had when he was a little boy. I hadn't realized that.

And then we walked home. He said he wanted to. We didn't talk very much, but Blake did say something a half-block away from our house that I have promised myself not to forget. You'll think I'm making this up. But I'm not. I know exactly where on our street this happened. You can see the tree from our living-room window.

This was early in spring. It wasn't a particularly nice afternoon. The leaves were just starting.

He stopped. And he looked at what light there was in a northern city, in April, on a mostly overcast afternoon. Not much. But there was enough to catch the tiny outlines of buds on the branches of a small, ordinary-looking tree. "Everything is so beautiful," he said.

And then we went home to tell his sister and his mother what the doctors had told him.

9

My grandfather was not a good golfer. He wasn't bad. He just wasn't particularly good.

I think my father was a slightly less good golfer. But he, also, wasn't bad. This was pretty much what we thought golf was for: to be okay at.

Golf did not figure prominently in our family. No more than bridge. Or the Art Gallery Ball. Or the Players' Guild. Or church. Golf was just part of the texture of middle-class life in Hamilton. And a father inviting a son to play golf was just something my mother felt fathers should do. Every now and then. Once in a blue moon. Before we all ended up dead and buried.

My mother was in her seventies when she started losing her marbles. Losing her marbles was her phrase. This proved to be a gently slow process, and as a result, there were several family stories that, by constant repetition, survived her dimming memory and hardened into crystalized, unassailable fact. The eighteen holes my father never played with his father constituted one of these. My mother used it as a kind of universal field theory to explain the family into which she had married. "Not once," she'd say, apropos of almost anything.

10

Blake had strong ideas about what worked in a story. And stronger ideas about what didn't.

At the time of his diagnosis he had a gig editing documentaries, and few things frustrated him more than having to cut a film with footage that had more detail than narrative. You could say he was professionally impatient with stories that didn't have stories in them. He had no time for unnecessary diversion.

He wasn't sure, for instance, that it mattered what my friends and I called the steps on the side of the escarpment. Giving them a name wasn't something most people did with steps.

Blake pointed this out after I'd read to him a passage about my memories of Jacob's Ladder. This was in one of those hospital rooms. I was sitting in one of those orange vinyl chairs. I get them all mixed up now. As usual, I'd worked at home for a few hours before coming in to Princess Margaret with his coffee in a Thermos and a bagel and cream cheese from the Harbord Bakery.

I was quite proud that the memory had come to me—"Out of the blue," I told Blake. We'd heard older kids use the name, I suppose. They'd heard even older kids. And so on. The original steps must have been built not too many years before my father was born, and in those days, in that neighbourhood you wouldn't have found many people who hadn't heard of Jacob's Ladder. I must have been nine when the old stairs were replaced with a more reliable-looking structure. And with the modern replacement, the old name vanished for some reason.

Jacob's Ladder was rickety. That was almost the only adjective ever used. The old wooden stairs zigzagged upward with the haphazard steepness of a vine finding its way up between outcroppings of limestone and clutches of big old roots. There were landings every twenty or so steps. They hadn't been level for decades.

As far as we were concerned, nothing much happened on those steps—other than older kids smoked and teenagers necked. This was the problem. In a movie it would be my gang of friends who were climbing Jacob's Ladder when we spied something unusual in the adjacent underbrush. Or maybe it would be only me—

there beneath a tumult of trees like the maples in John Hartman's painting—seeing something I could not believe I was seeing.

But that wasn't the case. It would be hard to pretend it was. The body was found on the escarpment, but not particularly close to Jacob's Ladder. And it was discovered more than ten years before I ever played in those woods. Children found John Dick's dismembered torso in March 1946.

The murder trial was big news in Hamilton—such big news that Evelyn Dick's name was occasionally the subject of playground jokes sixteen years later. I can vouch for that. It was as if those headlines in the *Hamilton Spectator* had been so lurid they remained, like the purple smoke of the coke ovens, like the fiery pour-offs at the open hearths, part of the city's atmosphere. We (meaning the kids on the playground at Earl Kitchener School) picked up the case long after the fact—as if what we could hear in the story that came down to us (chanted on playgrounds, whispered in polished corridors) was the dim residue of radio waves, evidence of a huge, prehistoric explosion.

You can imagine the flashbulbs. Evelyn Dick was found guilty of murdering her husband. But a new lawyer, the soon-to-be-famous J. J. Robinette, won her appeal. This was not the end of the story. Oh no.

The discovery of a baby's body changed things. To say the least. This was Evelyn's son. He was in concrete, in a suitcase, in a closet, in her Hamilton house. This did not encourage general belief in her innocence—as evidence: no shortage of the most obvious jokes possible about Evelyn Dick. Hamilton had never known a Hamilton story quite so sensational.

Blake had a knack for grasping the order of a story—like inventing a melody, like imagining a beat. It was not necessarily a predictable order—although when he edited documentaries he looked for the clearest narrative line he could find. But whether obvious or obscure, there was an order Blake saw quickly. More quickly than I did, anyway. He could discern the shape, whereas I was always scrolling forward or backward in time, trying to remember where I'd left off. He believed stories to be like melodies in this regard. They can rise and fall. They can call and respond. They can excite and calm. They can frighten and comfort. The possibilities are numerous. The one thing they have to do is begin and end.

On our summer drives to and from rented cottages when the kids were young, on our drives to and from Hamilton for swims at the pool, on our drives to and from Montreal to visit cousins, Janice (in charge of snack distribution and music selection from the passenger seat) frequently pointed out to Caroline, behind me, and to Blake, behind her, how composers, whether Beethoven or the Talking Heads, built things up and then, abruptly, stripped them down to almost nothing. These were the shifts of gear that kept things moving forward, she said. This was what gave things energy. It's what made them alive.

Stories could be all kinds of things—including bad. Blake had a real fondness for cheesy horror movies. But there was one thing about stories that was kind of obvious, Blake thought.

As the recipient of a highly unlikely and entirely unexpected diagnosis, he understood the power of the improbable. Things could come out of the blue. They just couldn't stay that way. They couldn't not become part of the story.

Pause.

"Shadow conceals—light reveals," said the director Josef von Sternberg.

A nurse had come in to change Blake's IV. He took another bite of his bagel and cream cheese.

I'd scrolled ahead on my laptop to find von Sternberg's quotation. I'd come across it while writing about my friend Alison Gordon. And I had to admit (Blake asked) I wasn't sure how Alison was going to fit in.

Von Sternberg continued: "To know what to reveal and what to conceal, and in what degrees to do this, is all there is to art."

"Exactly," Blake said.

The director of *The Blue Angel* and *Morocco* made this remark while demonstrating film noir lighting techniques at a lecture he gave in London in the late sixties. Or, I assume he made the remark in London. He often did at his lectures. It was the kind of thing people remembered.

At the lecture he used an attractive redhead as a model. She just happened to be in the audience that evening. You can see a picture of von Sternberg's London demonstration in film historian Kevin Brownlow's celebrated book *The Parade's Gone By*. That's Alison.

Alison Gordon was a writer, a radio producer, and the first woman baseball reporter in the American League. She'd been around the block once or twice. She made an excellent martini.

The band I'm in used to practise around her ex-husband's regulation-size snooker table in the basement of her east Toronto home. We didn't pay any rent. Alison just happened to enjoy having the band show up once a week. This went on for years—a routine of chips, guacamole, wine, and then music. And I only mention any of this because there was one band practice when Alison asked me to stay behind.

This was unusual. Alison was always pleased to see us arrive, but always happy to see us go. We never lingered.

Alison resisted the role of den mother to the band with some ferocity. But from time to time she intervened in our lives. She had strong opinions. If she felt something needed to be said, she said it. She could be blunt. She could be stern. And her disapproval wasn't something you wanted to encounter very often. Being asked to stay behind by Alison made me a little apprehensive, I have to say. Trepidation might not be too strong a word. But it turned out: she wanted to give me some advice. She'd had her own cancer scare.

I sometimes wondered if Blake's objection to a meandering story had to do with a boyhood coincident with *Star Wars* releases on VHS. In the story that held the same time slot in Blake's childhood that Sunday School held in mine, everything points toward and then moves away from the moment when Luke learns that Darth Vader is his father. The bible stories that marked my Sunday mornings did not march so directly and with quite so clean an edit toward Easter.

It wasn't just a matter of a plot line. Nobody was more critical than Blake of action movies that had nothing but action. It was aligning things so that everything belonged. If nothing was going to happen on Jacob's Ladder, then it made narrative sense to keep those stairs a little blurry and more in the background.

I told Blake that I liked the idea of the miraculous revealing itself in the ordinary. But he was, by the second year of being sick, understandably skeptical of miracles. The story of Jacob sleeping on a stone in the wilderness and dreaming of angels ascending a radiant staircase didn't have the resonance for Blake that it had for me.

When I told Blake that I was pretty sure I could remember the name of the slight, dark-haired boy under the clanging stairs at the back of Earl Kitchener Junior Public School, and that this particular boy lived not all that far from the bottom of Jacob's Ladder, Blake's expression didn't change. It didn't become less blank. And when I told Blake that the same boy would be murdered a few years later, Blake didn't see this as the development that I thought he would.

He may have been tired by then. There'd always been a dip in attention and an up-tick in irritation when Blake got tired. He said he wasn't sure that it mattered. I said it was probably time I got going.

He didn't think things tied together as neatly as his father seemed to want them to. He thought it entirely possible that things didn't tie together at all.

11

When Blake was attentive he was really attentive. His eyes widened—even when it was a story he'd heard a few times. If it was a story that held his imagination or caught the same frequency as his sense of humour, he leaned forward. He could be an excellent audience. But telling him that story that first time wasn't my idea. Certainly not.

Blake was thirteen, Caroline fifteen at the time. We had friends over for dinner, and one of them either forgot our kids were at the table, or decided that they were old enough to hear. We'd been talking about the Beatles, and about the effect psychedelic drugs had on their music. Our friend said, "Well, what about that time you played golf with your father?"

I remember Blake turning to me. I think it came as news to him that I'd ever played golf. "Yes," he said, "what *about* that time you played golf with Grandad?"

My father and I played (once, and only once) at the Hamilton Golf and Country Club. Which isn't in Hamilton. It's in the nearby town of Ancaster. It's a course that was planned and built by the great golf course designer Harry Colt in 1914, and it's known among students of the game's history as the course on which an extremely skilled and highly unorthodox player named J. Douglas Edgar set a PGA record in 1919 that stands to this day. No other player has come close to Edgar's achievement on that course—the same course that my father and I played fifty summers later. I was on LSD at the time—a detail Blake found highly amusing.

The opposite was just as evident. Blake reacted to boredom as if it were sleeping gas. If something didn't grab him he was inclined to drift. And now, given the amount of hydromorphone he was usually on, he would just fall asleep if he wasn't interested—as soundly as he used to, at the desk in his bedroom, when he had to do homework he didn't want to do.

You cut off his arms.

You cut off his legs.

You cut off his head.

I'm not even sure he was awake when I told him about Mrs. Dick.

12

My father's father was not a Hamiltonian by birth, but came from a different county in southern Ontario altogether. "Practically a foreigner," my mother used to say. Then roll her eyes. But Pappy came from the same kind of decent, proper background that produced the pretty young Hamiltonian he married. The ceremony took place at Centenary Church on Main Street just after the First World War. They made a handsome couple. But joyous outbursts of affection were not a family trait. Inevitably, this brought my mother to the subject of golf.

My great-grandfather was a bearded, stern-looking Methodist minister in a country parish somewhere in Prince Edward County—an appointment I remember only because it was how the middle name Blakely was introduced to our family. The custom in those days, so my father told us, was that a son born to the wife of a serving minister would be given, as a middle name, the name of the church's clerk of the session. Daughters were awarded no such honour. "We are all shocked to learn, I'm sure," my mother said.

My great-grandfather's obligation to Protestant custom couldn't have been one that future generations felt bound to honour. But that's how things have played out. My grandfather, my father, me, one of my two brothers, my son, my niece's son. We all have the same name. It's usually a middle name. It is for me. It was for my father and my son, but for both of them it was used as their first. They were Blake. Only when they encountered an institution—a hospital, for example—were they anything else.

My father wasn't what anyone would call loquacious. Nonetheless, he had his own rhetorical style.

He had a fondness for pieces of furniture the original utility of which had been erased by modernity: a bonnet box, a gout stool. He enjoyed equally antiquated turns of phrase. Stored in his memories of weekday hours spent in Hamilton classrooms and Sunday hours spent in Presbyterian pews were fragments of Tennyson and Genesis and Alfred Noyes and Isaac Watts. There was something he found amusing about being able to identify characters (Shadrach, Meshach, Abednego), locations (Naboth's vineyard, Belshazzar's palace) and objects (rumble seats, commodes, grape scissors) that nobody else remembered.

Religion was not a big part of family life when I was growing up—our attendance at church every week come hell or high water notwithstanding. Sunday school, choir, Cub Scouts, church pic-nics—these were obligations I took seriously, but no more seri-ously than swimming lessons at the Y or the chess club at school. My father was the same—an elder, an usher, a collection-taker, a calendar hander-outer, but I'm not sure I ever heard him say the name Jesus except in a hymn. And he wasn't much of a singer, believe me.

But that didn't mean we didn't know bible stories. The posses-sion of a working knowledge of burning bushes, bulrushes, and what happened to Lot's wife was what religion was for. We were led to believe. As a result I took my father's comprehensive knowledge of the bible for granted. Knowing who Jacob was and being famil-iar with his ladder was part of what I assumed to be an essential element of being a grown-up.

Five years after my father's death and a few months after my mother's, I discovered that his theological expertise came, not from ten thousand hours of sermons and study, but, for the most part, from *The Bible Picture Book*, which, in the general divvying up the contents of my parents' old house, came to me. My father's parents must have given it to him before he could be trusted with a fountain pen because it's my grandmother's cursive on the first page: *Blakely Macfarlane, 28 Duke St.* It's a handsome cloth-bound book of exactly one hundred bible sto-ries, each story faced with a full-page colour illustration. It was purchased, according to a fading stamp on the front endpaper, at Cloke's Bookshop, 18 King St. West. There was a time (approx-imately the span from my father's youth to my own) when every-body in Hamilton knew Cloke's. The store's gone now. You don't hear the name much anymore.

I made my discovery of *The Bible Picture Book* when my brothers and my sister and I were getting down to the final stages of emptying the house on Glenfern Avenue. The closing date was approaching, and a certain ruthlessness had entered the culling process.

The Bible Picture Book wasn't something I actually remembered from my own growing-up. I have no idea on what bookshelf in my parents' house it had been sitting for sixty years. So I was thinking of abandoning it. But then I noticed my father's name on the dedication page. Black ink. I wasn't sure I had another sample of Granny's writing. It would be something to pass on.

The title of each story in *The Bible Picture Book* was identical to the caption of each illustration. Rachel at the Well. Elijah and the Ravens. Jacob's Dream. And as I read each of them, something quite unexpected happened. I could hear my father's voice. He was saying: The Queen of Sheba visits Solomon. He was saying: Daniel in the Lion's Den. He liked being able to provide such arcane information. Moses smiting the rock at Meribah. Jericho falling. He was as old as Methuselah, he would say to his inquiring grandchildren.

My father treated certain words and turns of phrase like heirlooms. Were he to make reference to someone in Hamilton who could not be trusted, his standard description was "Oh, he's a snake in the grass." Sometimes a "snake in the grass" was also "a philanderer." When he employed these consciously old-fashioned terms it was never clear whether the irony in his voice was his making fun of the antique language or his making fun of himself for using it.

It was a tone of speech that was as recognizable to me as an accent. I felt the presence of a familiar ghost in the Nicholas Metivier Gallery in Toronto. I told John Hartman that it would be a pleasure to give him a tour of Hamilton. The same thing happens when I clear my throat. I sound just like my father.

13

Blake was twenty-nine years old. Sometimes I'd sit there and read to him from my laptop. "That's good," he'd say. Occasionally.

I thought that reading to Blake from what I was working on would be a good way for him to pass the time in the hospital. And it was true: passing the time in the hospital was an issue. It was something he pointed out, without bitterness. Just as an observation. He was sometimes in the hospital for weeks. People who could leave (so he told me one afternoon as I was leaving) had a fundamentally different experience of a hospital. Whether they were doctors or nurses or hospital administrators or social workers or meal-deliverers or janitors or therapists or visitors, they could all go home. And that meant they were in another universe. The trick to a horror movie set in a hospital, Blake thought, would be: no exteriors.

Blake had confidence about the jobs he took. He was sometimes scrambling, often learning new software on the fly. But there was something about Blake that, by the time he was twenty-four or so, conveyed to the people with whom he worked that if he didn't know a program, or a mixer, or a synthesizer at the moment, he would soon enough. He seemed to know where all this was heading.

But that wouldn't be for a while now. He had a to-do list in his head.

Directing a movie would be after getting better. That would be after getting back into shape. That would be after the travelling he wanted to do. He wanted to spend more time in Montreal.

His illness had delayed many plans. It was an unexpected interruption. When he was diagnosed Blake was co-producing an album with the Colombian-Canadian singer-songwriter Lido Pimienta. The album, *La Papessa*, won the 2017 Polaris Music Prize. He had done videos for the Montreal-based band Tasseomancy and for the Toronto singer Petra Glynt. We thought Blake was on his way. We just weren't sure where.

14

Had J. Douglas Edgar not been hit by a speeding car in Atlanta on a hot August night in 1921 (or, as seems more likely, had the thirty-seven-year-old professional golfer not been deliberately run over on West Peachtree Street by the husband of a woman with whom he was having an affair), Edgar might well have become what had been predicted of him.

Henry Vardon was a gruff, exacting Channel Islander. He was not abundant in his compliments, especially when it came to golf. He was the first pro to wear knickerbockers instead of long woollen pants, and his name still comes up whenever historians of the game argue about the best player of all time. Vardon was quoted in the sports pages saying that J. Douglas Edgar would one day become "the greatest of us all."

"I watched a good deal of Edgar's play," recalled the golf writer Bernard Darwin, "and never wish to see anything so consistently brilliant." But even if Edgar had not ended up sprawled at a disturbingly odd angle in the gutter of the 500-block of West Peachtree Street in Atlanta, Georgia, and had he lived to fulfill the promise people saw in his unusual swing, it's unlikely that any victories would have surpassed Edgar's achievement at the Hamilton Golf and Country Club on July 29 and 30, 1919.

When Edgar's final putt dropped into the cup of the eighteenth, just below the patio of the Hamilton clubhouse, he was sixteen strokes ahead of the runner-up. And the runner-up was not often a runner-up. The runner-up was a young amateur, already well known in golfing circles. His second-place finish notwithstanding, he'd shot a damn fine four rounds in Hamilton that weekend. Bobby Jones was a player who would come to be recognized (by the great golf writer Herbert Warren Wind, for one) as one of the greatest of the twentieth century.

J. Douglas Edgar beat Jones by the widest margin in PGA history. Edgar's record still stands.

In those days the galleries were modest compared to the galleries that follow pros around the course at tournaments today. The membership of the Hamilton golf club didn't care for the idea of hordes trampling over their fairways. There weren't many people who witnessed Edgar's astonishing feat.

But those who did would remember several things about it—other than his score, that is. They would remember that he walked with a happy jaunt. They would remember that sometimes—almost, it seemed, for his own amusement; almost, it seemed, for no reason other than to witness the beauty of the ball's perfect arc in the blue, cloudless sky—Edgar would curve a shot out over rough and woods until the force of the ball's spin would pull it back into the air above the fairway and drop it to the most advantageous of lies. He had consistently great distance. He had remarkable control. And the people who saw him play that weekend remembered another unusual detail. He whistled to himself all the way around.

15

As is true of many people who live in Toronto, my being originally from somewhere else is a small but determined point of pride that I reinforce whenever the opportunity arises. At the Metivier Gallery I was probably telling Hartman about my visits to my parents' old neighbourhood in Hamilton. That's my guess. I'd worked my stories up into a bit of a comic routine by then. "The streets time forgot," I'd say.

The Hamilton in which I grew up—the Hamilton of the 1950s and '60s—wasn't resentful of Toronto. We conceded certain points—and by "we" I mean the half dozen or so friends with whom I spent recesses on the crowded concrete playground of Earl Kitchener Junior Public School.

We didn't deny that Toronto had a great hockey team. Most of us were Maple Leafs fans. Toronto also had the annual, end-of-summer Canadian National Exhibition, and the Ex (to give credit where credit was due) had two roller coasters and a freak show. These were features of civic achievement we acknowledged.

But Hamilton had the steel companies. We had the Skyway Bridge. We had the mountain. We had Cootes Paradise and Burlington Beach. But above all—the clincher in any argument about which was the better city—we had the Hamilton Tiger-Cats. Sometimes the Ti-Cats. Sometimes the Cats. In stark contrast to the Toronto Argonauts, the Hamilton Tiger-Cats were, without doubt, the best team in the Canadian Football League, and frequently, by the end of November, we had the Grey Cup to prove it. Hamilton was (we were to a man agreed) much the superior city.

Years later, I occasionally wrote about Hamilton for various now-mostly-defunct Toronto-based magazines, and whenever I did I was encouraged to provide a few points of basic information about Hamilton for my readers. Most of whom lived in Toronto. It took me a few stories to realize that I resented this. I was from Hamilton, and some essentially non-Toronto part of me thought everybody should know where King and James was, what the mountain was, and who Evelyn Dick was. "Some context, please," an editor would scrawl, and in those days, they did. Scrawl. In margins. Of paper pages. Just like teachers.

"Hamilton, the capital of Canadian steel production during the middle six decades of the twentieth century, has a population of well over five hundred thousand. The Niagara Escarpment, a wooded ridge known locally as 'the mountain,' divides the municipality between older downtown neighbourhoods and the more recently developed upper quadrants."

Red check mark.

16

It's strange that my choice of career had such a strong association with swimming pools when my career has nothing to do with swimming. For reasons peculiar to Hamilton, magazine writing is a profession forever linked in my mind with the smell of chlorine.

After the YMCA on Saturday mornings I sometimes stopped in at my father's office to get a ride with him the rest of the way home.

Swim lessons had evolved into Aqua Club. This was a mostly miserable business that required racing dives, flip turns, and a lot of lengths in the green pool. I have no memory of ever wearing goggles. It must have been disconcerting for my father's patients to see the ophthalmologist's teary, red-eyed son peering at magazines through the blur of the Y's chlorine.

My father had current, mostly American magazines in his waiting room, although having good magazines in his waiting room wasn't characteristic of my father. He was more of an old *Reader's Digest* kind of doctor, really. But a good magazine subscription salesman must have noticed the low-hanging fruit of the six floors of doctors' offices in the Medical Arts Building. This was a lucky break for me. It was lucky in the same way it was lucky to be twelve years old when the Beatles hit. Because, as luck would have it, the four or five years when I stopped in at my father's office after the Y on Saturday mornings were particularly great years for *Life* and *Look* and *The Saturday Evening Post* and *Esquire*. The stories were fantastic. That's the word I would have used. And the graphics, amazing. They were probably never better displayed than when they were on the big, low wooden Mission-style table in my father's waiting room in the Medical Arts Building.

The magazines we had at home (across from the toilet, mostly) were much less likely to make anybody want to become a magazine writer.

But my parents had a few friends who, when they came over for a Sunday up at the pool, brought newspapers and magazines with them. This continued my association of great articles with chlorine.

Our friends left their reading material behind (like air mattresses and Coppertone) for general use. Up at the pool was where I first read Herbert Warren Wind (on golf), Roger Angell (on baseball), and David Halberstam (on football). I'm not sure when I began to wonder what it would be like to write stories for magazines, but the chances are good that I was wearing a bathing suit at the time.

Depending on the magazine, of course, a good subject for a magazine article in the 1980s was the return-to-the-hometown. It was adaptable. The return to home cooking. The return to comfortable décor. So long as freelance writers didn't go back to the well too often, it was a reliable pitch. I wrote my share. And when I did, for a Toronto readership, it often felt as if I'd discovered a city on the way to Niagara Falls that nobody had noticed. "Nobody knows anything anymore," was a complaint my mother often made of the modern world.

17

That's what Blake and I were talking about on one of those ordinary, too-bright days in the hospital. When the IV unit beeped. And the nurses came and went.

Blake always had two big cups of ice water on the go when the bed was raised. And we were talking—but not about whether my memory of what happened on that grey, long-ago playground was accurate. What Blake wanted to know was whether (accurate or not) it mattered enough for me to make a big deal of pointing it out.

I can see the room where our conversation took place: that bed, that chair. But what I can most clearly remember is that light—that volume of still, blank, hospital brightness. It could be a character in a story. It could, on its own, be the subject of a portrait.

18

She is a nurse. She has a beautiful face that is often described as handsome because her narrow features are so bold. She has straight, greying hair; a trim, neatly compact figure; and excellent posture. She speaks directly to camera.

This is black and white. And she is lit with the shadowy, in-between lighting of *Morocco* or *The Lady from Shanghai*.

It's her voice that is otherworldly. It's so mournful it feels like it carries the weight of the whole sad world. She would be speaking no more solemnly were she announcing the burning of continents, the rising of seas, the collapse of ecosystems. Her manner is compelling. She reads from the script in her hand. She says:

Interior. Cancer hospital. Day.

She continues reading the script. She says: A mother comes down the corridor.

She repeats this: A mother, you understand—a mother, in league with all mothers, comes down the corridor. It's the end of her turn at her son's bedside.

There is no dialogue, which is part of the scene's strangeness. The mother is a familiar face to everyone at the nursing station. She is someone who always says hello and goodbye as she comes and goes. Not this time. She doesn't look at anyone, and in return none of the nurses glance up from their paperwork or their computer screens to look at her. She moves quickly through the static white light of the hallway.

The corridor is lined with parked monitors, and hand sanitizers, and transport gurneys, and hampers for the gowns and gloves visitors take off when they leave.

She has no hat or snow boots. Her coat is thin brown cloth.

This sets her apart from the other visitors she passes in the hallway. They have come from outside. They have scarves and toques and down-filled parkas. They are dressed for bad weather. This is Canada. This is New Year's Day.

She steps out of the elevator on the ground floor.

Extreme close-up. Her eyes. And this is why visuals (a movie montage; the frames of a graphic novel) are so much more direct. Because you don't have to say "her sad eyes." You don't have to say: the saddest eyes you'll ever see.

In the hospital's ground-floor lobby there's the usual crowd. Even on a holiday. Slightly reduced in numbers, but pretty much the same as a regular weekday. People waiting. People arriving. Elevator doors opening. Closing. A couple of ambulance attendants. Some doctors. Some nurses. But on this occasion there's something unusual going on. Not that she notices as she makes her way toward the exit.

Everyone is preoccupied by the weather. Everyone is gaping in its direction. They look like they are witnessing an accident.

The sliding doors reveal the blizzard in gasps. It's horrendous out there.

In a city very familiar with bad winter weather, this weather has been the biggest item in the news for two days. It's unusual. Nobody's seen anything like it. Wind. Ice. Scary cold. The snow feels like pellets. It could rip your face off. It feels as if everything awful about a southern Ontario winter is being thrown at Toronto at once. The streets and sidewalks are choked with snowbanks that are hard as concrete.

The people who come through the revolving doors on the ground floor of Princess Margaret Hospital stamp off the snow and undo their hoods and take off their ski gloves to sanitize their hands—but not with the good humour with which Canadians usually accommodate the harshness of their climate. There isn't the usual understatement: "a bit nasty out there." There are no jokes: "those Syrian refugees must really be wondering what they've got themselves into." The wind is too biting for that. The temperature too bitter. It's more frightening than funny. This is what the end of the world will feel like.

A mother passes through the revolving doors of Princess Margaret Hospital. A mother, you understand. She is only wearing a thin brown coat. She is swallowed by the cold.

two

The Hamilton Tiger-Cats won the Grey Cup in 1963. The game was eight days after the assassination of President Kennedy, six days after the shooting of Lee Harvey Oswald, five days after Mr. Parsons explained what a cortège was, and three weeks after my bedroom was changed from the second floor, rear, to the basement, side, of my parents' house.

The death of President Kennedy is sometimes cited as the dawn of the television age. And that's surely what it was for me. We didn't go to school the day after. I was alone, sitting in front of our black-and-white RCA when Jack Ruby shot Oswald in that crowded corridor.

I never did become a sportswriter. My loss, I think. I preferred to have no particular area of specialization. I enjoyed immersing myself in the different worlds the freelance market threw at me. That's what I said. And it wasn't untrue. It was, however, another way of saying, I took what work I could. That's what all the freelance writers I knew did: we took the assignments that came along. Occasionally they were sports-related. I could see what drew me to the idea in the first place.

A game of football has a built-in narrative. There is no shortage of action. The drama of a game, or a season, or an athlete's life is well suited to sports columns, to magazine features, to books.

One of the fixtures of our life in Hamilton was the promi-nent role of the library—in our case, the Locke Street branch. My mother was a great champion of its use. Our visits were as regular as church, as swim class, as garbage day. Sports biographies, sports reporting, and sports fiction became my favourite reading. And so, naturally, I assumed that when I became a Pulitzer Prize–winning reporter my beat would be sports. A sport, to be precise. Covering the Tiger-Cats for the *Spec* was a future to which I devoted some serious daydreaming when I was in grade six.

The *Spectator* simultaneously covered and cheered for the Tiger-Cats and I assumed that a fringe benefit of a job on the Hamilton foot-ball beat would be having a first-name relationship with the team's great players. The quarterback, Faloney. ("Hey, Bernie, How'ya doin?") And Patterson, his great receiver. ("Hiya, Hal. How's the knee?")

I thought that being a star reporter covering the Hamilton Tiger-Cats and never having to do anything else, really, would be an excit-ing and, I was sure, richly rewarding occupation. It was attractive for all kinds of reasons. Slang being one. Incomplete sentences another. But over time (and I simply would not have believed this possible when I was ten or eleven years old) my devotion to the Tiger-Cats became less obsessive than it had been. There were other channels, as things turned out.

Some things stay with you. It's not clear why they do. Some stay on the surface of memory—like literal representations in a paint-ing of a house, or a playground, or a hillside of woods. These are the stories that I repeat to myself: the time a teenaged girl opened a back door; the time a quarterback and his receiver got their signals crossed; the time a son's bedroom exploded with light.

I'm not sure that these memories are any more accurate for being repeated. In fact, the opposite may be true. It may be that each time a memory is called to mind I adjust it, slightly, to make it a better fit for the fragments of recollection I piece together as my life. But less true. If there is an order to things it's probably not what I think it is.

What I told Blake was that one of the humbling aspects of being born seven years after the end of the Second World War is that all the clichés about the baby boom generation are true—or, at least, truly relevant to actual events in my actual life. This can be disconcerting. Even embarrassing. But yes, as a matter of fact, in the fall of 1963 the world did begin to change in ways that could not be imagined. It really was the dawn of a new age. At least, for me it was. The tone of Hartman's painting (the bursts of brightness coming through the darkness) are particularly evocative of that particular autumn.

Insofar as it's possible for a huge portrait to be accidentally hanging in the living room of the portrait's subject, that's what happened in the case of the Hartman painting. Its presence was as out of sequence with the evolution of our Toronto house as a comet. And what I think happened is this: I think I said that I could probably write something about the painting. I said this to Nicholas Metivier, who is the owner of the gallery in Toronto where Hartman shows. And the reason I said this was because I didn't know what else to say. "Okay," he suggested. "We'll lend it to you." This wasn't what I expected to happen.

And what I noticed when I first sat down in our living room to spend a few minutes looking at the painting Nicholas Metivier's art installers had delivered and hung was how well Hartman captured the trees. They're just as I saw them from my upstairs bedroom.

As a result of the insertion of my youngest brother into the internal geography of 25 Glenfern Avenue, I was shifted to a small, recently finished bedroom in the basement when I was eleven years old. It featured fake-wood panelling, a closet with a sliding door, and a linoleum floor. The ceiling was comprised of white squares that, at a later stage of my development, proved to be excellent hiding places for *Playboy* and, a little later still, a water pipe. Compared to the four other bedrooms in the house, mine felt very new.

The biggest change, however, was that my new bedroom had no window-full of trees. The view from the second floor, rear, of my parents' house was largely a view of the woods—mature maple, mostly. The woods were on the steep slope of the Niagara Escarpment, and this gave my perspective (bed, beside window; sill, eye level) an unusual tilt. It wasn't the normal way to see big trees.

By day, you could see the trees behind the trees from my bedroom window—just as Hartman has painted them. At night they joined together, moving as if some huge, lazy force was rippling underneath their darkness.

Most of my memories of the view from the second-floor window are general—as if it was unusually intriguing wallpaper. But I do recall a few instances (chicken pox; firecracker night) when I can see myself sitting on the side of my bed, my nose on the metallic smell of that screen. My last specific memory of that bedroom is a Saturday evening in October 1963. I'd been sent to my room early because I'd gone to a Tiger-Cats football game at Civic Stadium on my own that afternoon.

"You did *what*?" my mother wanted to know. And that's the last time I remember sitting there, in that bedroom, looking out that window at that hillside of big old trees.

The window in my new basement room didn't look out to anything. It was the size of a Monopoly board. It was at ground level. Literally ground level. There were higher peonies.

This was the dawn of a new age. But when I think of all the changes that would follow that autumn, I don't first think of Walter Cronkite wearily removing his reading glasses to look up from the bulletin he had just been handed to make the sad announcement. I picture my new bedroom. I'm getting ready to go across the street to watch the Grey Cup. It was the same November.

The Cats were playing the Lions in Vancouver. The championship is remembered for a late hit that sidelined Vancouver's great running back, Willie Fleming. As far as the entire province of British Columbia was concerned it was a fully intentional, game-changing piece of football nastiness. Hamiltonians argue that Angelo Mosca, the 6'4", 275-pound defensive tackle who landed like a ton of bricks on the already-down Fleming, was in the air when the whistle was blown.

And how deep do feelings run? Still? Well, consider this.

Joe Kapp was the quarterback of that Vancouver team, and he and Mosca were reunited at a Canadian Football League charity luncheon. This was *forty-eight* years later, and here, I have to admit, I cannot improve on Wikipedia. "After both players traded words, event host Ron James invited both players to make a peace gesture. Kapp jokingly presented Mosca with an ornamental flower he had picked at his table. When Mosca emphatically refused it, Kapp tried to shove it in his face. Mosca swung his cane at Kapp in retaliation, hitting him in the head. An irate Kapp then knocked Mosca down to the floor with a pair of punches and kicked him, before turning to the stunned attendance and shouting, 'Sportsmanship! That's what it's all about folks, sportsmanship.'"

It was quite the Grey Cup. I watched it in a television room across the street. This was a friend's house. He had an older sister. He also had a younger sister, but it was the older sister Hartman's painting brings to mind.

The painting only suggests my parents' neighbourhood. But it's suggestion enough. On one of the mornings I sat in front of it with my coffee, before the bright day began, I remembered something that I knew as a child but had lost track of somehow over the years. All those houses were personalities. The Gibsons. The Vances. The Wards. The Duncans. The Boothes. The Goldbergs. The Ewens. The Hemings. The Harrisons. The houses themselves were characters—as if they, with their forthcoming doors and expressions of windows, were members of the families who lived in them.

For instance: when we were all trying to picture the inside of Donny's house (Where were the stairs? Where was the landing? Where was his sister's bedroom? Where was his mother?) I was probably pretty accurate, even though I'd never been inside it. He lived eight blocks away. But Donny's house was the same age, same size, same general design, and same east-west axis as the house across the street from ours, and I'd been inside the house across the street a million times. It's where I was going to watch the 1963 Grey Cup. They were probably the same builder.

I can show you where they both are in the painting. I can even show you where, in the painting's imaginary space, I picture the back door. I was standing there on a Saturday afternoon late in the November of 1963. As far as I knew, the only thing on my mind was football.

After I pushed the bell, and after what was an unusually long response time, it was my friend's older sister who answered. Everyone was already upstairs watching the pre-game warm-up.

Jo-Anne had come to the door before. But something had shifted in me, or was about to shift, or was shifting, and it was the first time Jo-Anne came to the door the way Jo-Anne came to the door that particular day. Not that she did anything or said anything that was unusual. It was just: there she was.

Jo-Anne had a boyfriend her parents didn't know about. He was a few years older than she was and he spent a lot of time in his parents' garage a couple of blocks away working on a Harley-Davidson. It was an old police bike, with one of those big single saddles. The slow chug of the engine sounded like it was coming through a bass amp.

Jo-Anne's secret boyfriend was ridiculously handsome. He was trimly built, almost small. He wore white T-shirts with grease on them. He had an off-kilter grin. He actually looked like James Dean. So you can guess what Jo-Anne looked like. She must have been fifteen.

Her ponytail swayed as she led me up the stairs to the television room.

2

It was our mother who told my sister, my two brothers and me how to behave. How to hold a knife and fork. How to sit still in the car. How to not-fidget in our pew at Melrose United Church. How to cover our mouths when we yawned. How to say excuse me as required. How to accommodate the wishes of others. How to be appreciative. In short, how to be polite.

These lessons occupied a significant part of our early upbringing. I still feel my mother's elbow in my side if I am slow to rise when a woman arrives at a table at which I am seated. "Chivalry's last gasp," she mutters, when I sit back down.

My father preferred to show by example how to avoid being (his term) a lout. "Were you born in a barn?" was about as specific as he got in his criticisms of our domestic and social insufficiencies. He didn't instruct us, exactly. The only piece of advice he ever gave me was that when I was in a fight (a semi-regular occurrence among boys at Earl Kitchener Public School in the early 1960s) I should, as a first step in my defense, bloody the other fellow's nose. Those were his words. Bloody. Fellow. And like a lot of the words he used, they had a cordial quality. They conjured a time of gentlemanly fisticuffs very different from the messy squabbles of pushing and tripping and swearing that were what playground fights had become. Popping somebody in the nose with a closed fist seemed a bold opening gambit.

As to our day-to-day manners, though, my father didn't have much to say. We could watch him if we wanted to learn how to conduct ourselves. And this, in consort with our mother's more hands-on approach to etiquette, seems to have worked. There was an acquiescence to accepted custom in my father's eyes that, judging by the portrait of me by John Hartman that hangs in our living room, is also visible in mine.

This instinct to be polite under almost any circumstances was one of the characteristics of the WASP middle class that Blake was never sure about. He was not so beholden to convention as his forebears. We pretty much gave up suggesting what he might wear to weddings or family birthdays by the time he was thirteen. He had his own style. It often included mismatched socks and unusual sunglasses. But the slightly complicating factor for Blake was that along with the rebellious glint of a young man, the gentility of his grandfather was apparent in his eyes, too. In the hospital, Blake could be impatient. Who wouldn't be? He could be extremely grumpy. And why not? He was poked and examined and awakened in the night to change IV drips or check his vitals. But almost always he was polite. These are things that are passed along. I think of my father whenever I take off a glove to shake somebody's hand on a winter day.

I was never confident that I inherited my father's authenticity, however. Although I imagine he felt the same way about his father. Edwardian etiquette becomes more ironic the further away in time you get from Edward.

"The Seventh," my parents would have chimed in.

3

My answer to John Hartman's request that I show him around Hamilton could have been taken as an unreliable reflex. I'd love to. Absolutely. It would be a pleasure.

These are not iron-clad contracts—as is generally understood in the quarters where promises such as these are more small talk than anything. I worry sometimes that I am more naturally disposed to being polite than actually helpful. But in this instance I meant what I said. It would be a pleasure.

My discoveries of Hamilton were a favourite conversational topic of mine at the time. And by discoveries I don't mean the solving of mysteries, or the revealing of scandals, or the unearthing of crimes. I mean ordinary things discovered while out for a walk while visiting my widowed mother, who had by then become a sweet elderly citizen—cheerful, still physically healthy, and flummoxed (a word she liked) by her diminishing mental faculties. She passed from a long-established holding pattern to slow deterioration in lockstep with the house in which she'd lived for more than sixty years.

The old place left a pleasant, comfortable impression on short-term visitors. As did my mother. It took a while (an overnight would do it) for a guest to realize how things actually were.

Most of the homes in the neighbourhood had been built in the 1920s and a number of them were much like ours: vaguely Arts and

Crafts. "Very vaguely," my mother used to say. The front veranda had a fieldstone foundation. The house itself was two substantial but not exactly soaring storeys made of wood and a local corrugated red brick. The windows, of which there were many, were draughty in winter and festooned with awnings in the summer. The trees around the property were mature. Maples, mostly. So it would be called quaint today.

"Quaint?" I can hear the outrage. "Give me strength," was something my mother often said.

However stubbornly the middle class resists the forces of the universe, entropy is entropy. It had been thirty years since the house had been at the top of its game. Nothing beyond toast and instant coffee had been attempted in the kitchen for ages.

When I visited Hamilton my mother and I always had one Scotch and water before dinner. We ordered the same takeout over and over. We watched DVDs we'd seen before. There was something soothing about all this—an absence of event to which I found myself looking forward. No platelet count to worry about. No hemoglobin to be up. To be down. In the evenings I went for walks.

What came as a surprise in Hamilton was how clear and, at the same time, how distant my childhood felt. The light through the canopy of maple, the leathery smells of autumn, the shifting gears of the buses climbing Beckett Drive—these were the kinds of details that you might encounter in a dream of a place you haven't been for a long time. They feel so familiar you can't imagine how you let them slip your mind.

These distinctly West Hamilton sights and smells and sounds reminded me how central they'd been to our lives. A house doesn't often remain headquarters to a family for as long as my parents' did. It was the only one they ever had. A neighbourhood doesn't often change so slowly.

I'd always thought a long-ago childhood was my father's specialty. My adolescence was modern—modern as Keds, and Frisbees, and Channel 7, Buffalo. It continued to feel youthfully up-to-date long after it actually was because my father lay such natural claim to ancient history. Somewhere in his otherwise undemonstrative voice were the villains and heroes of the G. A. Henty and C. S. Forester novels he'd read in his bedroom in the old Duke Street house in pre-war Hamilton. He never quite forgot Room A27 at Westdale Collegiate. He still had fragments of "The Highwayman" and "The Lady of Shalott" memorized and at the ready.

I considered my childhood to be unremarkable by comparison. "And that," I can hear my mother saying, "is how clueless you are." My mother had her views on how miraculously fortunate it was for anyone to be have been born healthy, comfortable, and Canadian in the middle of the twentieth century. "You don't know how good you got it, kiddo."

4

Paint makers once created darkness with charred ivory. What resulted was the black you'd expect of so grim a process. If you were painting the flip side of my untroubled growing up, you'd use a colour like it. If, for example, you wanted to paint the residential school to which we, the well-meaning congregants of Melrose United Church, sent gifts at Christmas, you'd use it. If you were painting the industrial sludge that collected at the bottom of Hamilton Harbour, you'd use it. If you were painting crimes like these you'd want to use a black as awful as the burnt tusks of slaughtered elephants.

These days iron oxide is the most common foundation of colour's absence in paint. Black's components are bound with lubricant and minerals, and when the compound is thinned with linseed oil it can be used on the horizon to describe the haze of distance. When lightly but smoothly applied (like the underside of autumn clouds over Lake Ontario), black can be a metaphor for the uncertainty of distant memory. It can also evoke the mists of time.

You cut off his arms.

You cut off his legs.

You cut off his head.

How could you?

The huddle of boys I'm remembering under the back stairs, clang, clang, happened only a few weeks before Mr. Parsons had to drum how to spell "assassination" into our thick skulls ("double s, double s" underlined in red ink).

It was noisy at recess. It was like being inside a hedge full of birds.

Mr. Parsons' black shoes. The bottom clang.

5

On December 27, 2017, our family—meaning Caroline, Blake, Janice and I—went to the Art Gallery of Ontario. I hadn't been to the AGO since the day of Blake's diagnosis. But an exhibit dedicated to the work of Guillermo del Toro, the film director, had opened and del Toro was a big star in Blake's firmament. We all wanted him to see the show.

Pan's Labyrinth had been released in 2006, *Hellboy* two years before that, and Blake was a fan: the same love of fantasy and B movies and animation and comic books. "Screenplay," del Toro once said, and it is something I can perfectly imagine Blake quoting to me, "is the toughest form of writing . . . because you need to be in the present tense. You need to be describing things as they occur."

Del Toro is an artist who has followed a zigzagging path to becoming a director. Things didn't follow a sequence—at least not a standard sequence, and Blake admired that. Del Toro worked as an actor and a makeup artist and an animator and a special-effects creator and a writer and a producer—a route that only in hindsight looked ingeniously plotted toward an Academy Award for best picture.

Going to the AGO was something we used to do a lot on holidays with Caroline and Blake when they were kids. Especially in that week between Christmas and New Year's, when winter closed in and we hunkered down together in our tall, narrow, mortgaged-to-the-hilt red brick house. We were, I think it's fair to say, a happy family. Money never seemed to stay very long in our bank account, but we generally had enough coming in to cover what was going out. Janice started her own design business. She wrote a book about colour. I took on whatever magazine gigs came my way.

Back then, when people who were our parents' age asked, as they sometimes did (with an air of amused amazement), why our house was where it was, we said we liked living downtown. This was quite true. But really our house was where it was for the obvious reason. It was in one of the rundown, bikes-on-the-front-porch, dream-catcher-in-the-window, part student housing, part rooming house, part cool professor, part old Portuguese couple Toronto neighbourhoods that, in the 1970s and even into the 1980s, we could (just barely) afford. This was a lifetime ago, and although this was not quite so obvious then as it seems now, we were part of what was coming. Our property's value increased tenfold in thirty years. We've never moved.

The AGO was close enough for us to walk to in even the worst of winter-holiday snowstorms. We had our route.

When they were kids, Caroline and Blake would choose the painting they liked the most and the one they liked the least of any room in the gallery we entered. Janice invented this game. And it turned out to be a good one.

My favourite was always Édouard Vuillard's *The Widow's Visit* (1898, oil on paper mounted on wood). It's a painting I discovered when Janice and I were at the University of Toronto and I'd got up the nerve to ask her out. We went to the AGO one afternoon. And if anyone is wondering what to do on a first date, may I suggest: an art gallery.

The Widow's Visit is not very big, not very colourful, and, on the face of it, not a whole lot of fun. A blurry portrait of three old ladies in a slightly too small middle-class Parisian apartment was not a crowd-pleaser as far as our kids were concerned. But it is the light on the apartment's back wall, coming from a window the viewer cannot see, that makes the painting so great. I'd say. Look. But it was a hard sell. An acquired taste, I'd say —which is what my father said to me about buttermilk.

The best show ever with the kids was Keith Haring. Blake was nine. "A light bulb going off," Blake said.

So of course Blake would want to go to the Guillermo del Toro show at the AGO. But it wasn't easy for him to go anywhere by that December.

He was at home. He was being hit with bouts of pain that roamed unpredictably around his body.

Blake had almost no patience for the word "journey." So, you should bear that in mind when I tell you that his journey began with bouts of pain he couldn't explain and which (by the time he called me from the apartment on Bloor Street he shared with some musician friends) were becoming scary. That was the first such call, and it was the first of many trips to hospitals. So it's not as if the bouts of pain were a new development. What was new by the December of the del Toro show was their frequency. Sometimes—especially at night, for some reason—he could not find a position that afforded him any relief, no matter how much hydromorphone and Tylenol and cannabis oil he took and how carefully we followed his instructions about arranging pillows and heat pads and ice packs.

One night the pain wouldn't stop. I won't try to pretend I have any idea what it felt like. But I will tell you what being the parent of a child in pain like that felt like: it felt like my nerves were exploding. I remember standing in front of him and crying—full-throated sobbing—because there was nothing we could do to help.

Blake was standing beside his bed in T-shirt and sweatpants because he thought standing might be better than lying down. It wasn't. I didn't know what to do. So I hugged him.

He was standing with his arms around me, mine around him. He let me take some of his weight. And he said: "That feels better."

He was the one who gave the position a name. He'd call in the middle of the night sometimes that month. I was two floors up, phone beside the bed. He'd say: "Sorry to wake you." He called it Jacob's Ladder.

There were also times during this same period when he felt okay—as in, not all that bad. We didn't treat these episodes of okayness as anything special, really. We regarded them more as status quo than respites. They were how Blake would feel all the time when he was better. And so, when his sister and his mother encouraged him to go to the AGO show, it wasn't in the spirit of a special occasion. For the four of us to go to the Guillermo del Toro show in the week between Christmas and New Year's was the most ordinary thing in the world. The only unusual aspect of Janice's and Caroline's idea was that, in the storyline from which Blake's illness had steered us, it would have been Blake who was doing the encouraging. In fact, he probably would have already seen it, reporting to us at the dinner table how much fun it was to wander through the curios of del Toro's Dickensian interiors and what a surprise to come across an actual pianist playing an actual grand piano (Satie, Chopin, Schumann) in one of the show's last mysterious rooms. Two weeks later we tracked down the pianist to play at Blake's service.

Blake had always been incapable of keeping his enthusiasms to himself. This was especially true at dinner—a daily ritual on which Janice insisted. As kids, Blake and Caroline would tell us about movies or books or bands. So I am sure that in 2004, when he was seventeen, Blake would have talked about del Toro directing *Hellboy*, based on the graphic novel by Mike Mignola. It was right up Blake's alley. But I have no actual memory of this happening. I wasn't all that clear on who del Toro was when Janice came into my office two days after Christmas and said we were all going to the AGO, and I said that maybe I'd stay home and keep working, and she said: We're all going to the AGO.

Blake had a lot of horror movies on various hard drives. On top of which: he had leukemia. Improbable plot twists were not necessarily incorrect. Blake felt.

What he was suspicious of—what he really strongly objected to—was literary display. It was for him the written equivalent of what in the world of real estate transaction is known as "fluffing" or "staging"—the cluttering of an interior with throw pillows and vases of flowers in order that prospective buyers don't see what's actually there. And I could see that Blake had a point. It did seem suspiciously literary, in what I was reading to him—on my laptop, in that hospital room—that things tied together as they did.

Blake sometimes employed an intently blank expression. This expression didn't actually involve the raising of an eyebrow. But it had the same effect. Because what I told him was this.

The schoolyard chant about Evelyn Dick was being recited under the clanging stairs by a boy (slight, dark hair) who would, it so happened, be murdered himself a few years later.

Red check mark.

6

It wasn't all that long before my mother died that Hartman and I agreed we would get together for a tour of Hamilton. Absolutely. I'd love to. It would be a pleasure. But spring and summer slipped by, and eventually, there we were: in the fall, on the gravel driveway of my parents' old home. The leaves were still splendid. Perhaps because the sunshine was only intermittent, I don't remember the brightest colours Hartman ended up using when he worked on his painting of that day.

At that time—the time you can see in the painting—Blake was in the first year of treatment. My wife, our daughter, Blake's girlfriend Effy, and I were by then all familiar with two or three oncology wards in Toronto, a few infectious disease clinics, and several Toronto emergency rooms. A ruptured appendix and a rare fungal infection had complicated things that were already complicated enough with Blake's cancer. There were viruses he picked up in the hospital and infections he may have picked up from the takeout he ordered (to my amazement) when he was in hospital. "Are you allowed to do that?" I asked. Blank stare from Blake in response.

There were operations. On his abdomen. On his shoulder. He couldn't move his arms for a while. We had to, for him. There were rounds of antivirals. There were surgical wounds that wouldn't heal. There was a hernia that grew and grew, and how Blake hated that paunch. There were a lot of painkillers. There was chemo. There were whacks of antibiotics.

He'd been healthy and fit all his life and then suddenly, he wasn't. He totally wasn't. It was like fucking Job. That's how it seemed sometimes, and it was never just Job. Always *fucking* Job. By the time Blake was told that the fungal infection he had somehow picked up was extremely dangerous and extremely rare, he said: Why am I not surprised? I was there once when a young doctor (more or less the same age as Blake) stood beside his bed, flipped through his chart, and said, "Wow."

Platelets and hemoglobin became subjects of daily conversation. We talked about them, asked about them, wondered about them, read about them, worried about them. We were learning about the weird emotional cycles caused by steroids. We were adjusting to the waxing and waning of Blake's energies.

And then things took a turn. This was around the time of my mother's death. This was five months before the day you can see in Hartman's painting.

Blake's counts were not good. Definitely not good. On the day of my mother's funeral, Blake was back in Princess Margaret Hospital. There were doctors and nurses around his bed a lot of the time. He was extremely thin.

The translucence of his hands made me think of polished statuary. And that's as far as I would allow that avenue of thought to go. It was something I did a lot in those days—consciously steer away from obituary pages in newspapers, sorrowful music, movies with sad endings, statues of Mary with her grown, dead son in her arms. I tried to avoid anything that contradicted what I was looking for when I stepped into Blake's room. Sometimes the things

I hoped to see (energy, humour) were there and sometimes they weren't. But I never took the pose of the *Pietà*'s Jesus as Blake's natural state although that was sometimes exactly what he looked like. Really exactly.

Even when he was pale as polished Carrara marble Blake had a confidence in which I believed. Dogged, determined, defiant— these three words were part of a private ritual I conducted every morning. They were the description of Blake on which I insisted to myself—especially when the disease seemed to be dictating different terms.

Dogged, determined, defiant. Dogged, determined, defiant. I began this silent prayer when I was making coffee. Dogged, determined, defiant. Every morning had to begin with those words. I never told anyone this. Especially not Blake.

"It's not my time," he said to us on the day of my mother's funeral. There was something so matter-of-fact in his tone of voice that we all believed it. So his sister stayed with him in the hospital in Toronto. They'd always been close. They'd always been pals.

And Janice and I drove to Hamilton. I could show you in the painting where my mother's funeral took place. And Blake was right. It wasn't his time.

7

John Hartman's preoccupation is light. He thinks about it a lot when he is beginning a painting. Mostly he thinks about light by mixing his colours on a large, glass palette and picturing their effect. He pictures what they will be like immediately, of course. He has to predict how they will resonate with other colours at the instant of their application to the surface of a painting. Even a limited palette can, by juxtaposition of pigment, produce a wild, kaleidoscopic composition. But the artist has also to consider: What will the effect of the colours be with some saturation of the paint's oil into the fabric? With time? With the white light of the gesso shining back through the translucence of age?

If a painting draws you into the world it creates, there is reason to suspect that you are in the presence of a good one. And this is something I should point out about living with a work of art. What I've discovered is that not only does a painting create what Hartman calls imaginative space, it draws you into that space.

Were you to ask me what it is that makes good art good (Édouard Vuillard: *The Widow's Visit*) I'd sputter for a while but eventually I'd say, It asks questions. Not that there are not other considerations. Technique. Execution. Composition. Skill. There's a checklist. And I'm not suggesting there shouldn't be. But if you are looking at a painting that doesn't ask questions there's a pretty good chance you're standing in front of what my father would call "a dud."

For example, I wondered: Why, when Hartman depicts the city of Hamilton in the background with such thick intensity, does he sketch the neighbourhood in the middle ground so economically? This wasn't a criticism. It was a question—not necessarily a question with an answer, but a question that became part of my experience of looking at the painting.

Hartman's approach immediately raises another question: Why does it work? In a more literal world, the middle ground would be more filled-in than the background, not less.

Of course, nobody sees this painting the way I see this painting—which makes my judgment of it of no use to anyone. But when you are able to spend a good deal of time looking at a work of art (sometimes in natural light, sometimes in bright electric clarity) you do get drawn in. Believe me, you do. You can look at it from across the room and you can look at it up close. You can move around. You can stay still for as long as you want, unhurried by the current of a crowd at an art gallery. You can daydream about it. You can enter its imaginative space.

Were Hartman's painting not a painting at all, but a panel in a graphic novel, the boughs of mature deciduous trees, in October, just to the left of my head, would be understood by experienced graphic-novel readers to be the representation of the subject's wistful memories. This isn't quite a portrait of an old man, but we're getting there. Autumn is what the picture is about.

Hartman has used D. L. Stevenson oil paints (a Canadian company, he is quick to point out) since he was an art student in the early 1970s. Once Canada's leading manufacturer of fine-arts paints, D. L. Stevenson appealed to Hartman's quiet, steady nationalism. But nationalism wasn't sufficient on its own—a practicality that seems very Canadian to me. D. L. Stevenson is good paint and he's accustomed to it. Painting light is tricky enough without having to think about being patriotic.

Hartman respects elements of the artistic process that he can't entirely explain: the moments of inspiration that somehow—unheralded by anything you can put a finger on—change everything in a painting. But he also has a pragmatic side. He has a steady, show-up-at-the-studio-every-day approach to creativity. And he has great respect for his tools. He pays a lot of attention to them. He pays a lot of attention to brushes, to palette knives. To paint. Sometimes I use a magnifying glass in our living room to see what he is thinking.

8

What I didn't tell Blake was that entering the painting's imaginative space was an opportunity for me to enter another world for a while—a world that was comforting because it wasn't the present. So I'd sit in the living room. So I'd look at the painting. I'd remember things, which was a change from worrying about things.

I'd come upstairs to my office (second floor, front, Caroline's old bedroom) and work for a few hours. Then I'd pack a breakfast for Blake (a blueberry muffin or bagel and cream cheese from the Harbord Bakery, a smoothie made by his mother) and arrive at his room at Princess Margaret by ten or so, and every now and then, I'd read him what I was working on. I never did tell him about the praying.

But I did admit to him (in that white light, on that fourteenth floor of that shiny, bright hospital) that I was superstitious—superstitious enough to know that I would never, not in a million years, have made up a story about the boy under those clanging back stairs at Earl Kitchener. I do the same with ladders. I don't walk under them if I can help it.

The superstition came from Mrs. Simms. I'm sure of it. Mrs. Simms was our babysitter. She was always the first of two or three regulars my parents asked. She was what, in those days, people called "an older woman." Meaning, I suppose, that she was in her late fifties. She had white hair. And older-woman shoes. She was Welsh—as she frequently reminded us.

There. You see.

That's what I'm talking about. Those are the things I found myself remembering. I had not thought of Mrs. Simms—certainly not by name—in years. In decades, actually. But while looking at Hartman's painting, I thought of her. Her apron. Her sore hip.

Her superstitions and turns of phrase. "Up the wooden hill." I told Blake that's what she used to say when it was bedtime.

There was a Mr. Simms. I remember him as wizened by a life that included hard work, a war, more hard work, and a lot of cigarettes. I think he worked for a plumbing company. There was a son, Earl, who quit high school to work at Stelco. There was a teenage daughter named Susan who showed up from time to time when her mother was at our house.

Susan was an early warning to me about the unsettling role girls were going to play in my life. My attention to her, and her amusement at it, went unnoticed by everyone else. She was four or five years older than I was, and I must have been nine or so. She had dark, teased hair often wrapped in a chiffon scarf. She wore pointy black shoes. She looked like a pop singer: the kind with boyfriends who were back, or away, or dead in a motorcycle accident. It was as if Susan Simms had a scent—but not exactly that, somehow. It was more like a shift in the atmosphere around her.

But when I told Blake about Mrs. Simms (and Mr. Simms, and Earl, and Susan) I could see that, were it not for the various IV drips and PICC lines and monitors to which he was hooked up, he would have actually waved his hands in front of his face as if whisking away mosquitoes. This is a universal signal among film editors.

It's not that Blake thought movies superior to books. He'd been transformed one summer holiday at a cottage we rented in Georgian Bay. Almost overnight, he was changed from being a little boy who disliked reading to a little boy who walked around (from cottage, to outhouse, to sleeping cabin, to dock) with his nose in a book. This was due largely to *Harry Potter*.

Chinua Achebe, Toni Morrison, Octavia E. Butler, Haruki Murakami, Fyodor Dostoevsky are on his bookshelf. (I just looked; so are a lot of books I don't know at all, most of them graphic novels.)

But Blake was of the view that a good movie script tended to have a focus in its storyline that a few books he could mention would have done well to emulate. It wasn't so much that he was drawn to the intricacies of plot. It was the energy of narrative that he liked. He liked the feel of a story's pulse.

"But that's what I mean," I told him.

I can't now be sure at what stage of his illness this conversation took place. But because I associate it with an easterly view from a hospital window (the grid of Toronto splayed out below us), I think it must have been in the fall of 2017, around the time of the stem-cell transplant. Fourteenth floor. Princess Margaret. Caroline was an almost perfect match—which is not often the case with a sibling donor, and which was fantastically good news. Still, it's a fraught process at the best of times and had already involved a few tense days in the ICU. But we were back on the fourteenth floor, and what I told Blake was that even though my memory of that huddle of boys under those clanging stairs is not clear, and even though, I will admit, the identity of the boy who was reciting that old Hamilton schoolyard chant was the kind of connection a fiction writer might dream up, I knew I wasn't inventing it.

It must have been something Mrs. Simms said. I told Blake I wouldn't have ever made up that story about that boy under those stairs. That's because telling a lie about the dead is asking for bad luck.

9

My parent's swimming pool is as central to Hartman's painting as I am. It's someone else's pool now, and because I haven't been back since the autumn day that can be seen in the painting I don't know if the new owners have changed it in any significant way. I'm sure they must have.

Its size made people think that it was older than it was. There was nothing kidney-shaped or plastic-lined about it. It was good old poured concrete: just as permanent as, and much the general shape of, the foundation of a small church. It was long enough for adult swimmers to swim proper lengths, and wide enough for younger swimmers to learn to kick with paddle boards, and deep enough for proud young divers of flawless jackknives ("Dad, watch this!") to not hit the bottom.

The pool was surrounded by old trees and by shadowed gardens and the backs of brick houses, several of which were actually closer to the water than was the back of my parents' house. This isolation gave the pool a reclusive, glamorous quality. As further evidence of the property's burnished antiquity, an old fieldstone wall ran the length of the pool's south side.

That's how we used the term: the pool. It didn't mean only the volume of water. When we said "the pool" we meant the whole upper lot: the deck, the cabana, the filter room, the changing room, the hedges, the fence, the hula hoops, the toy sailboat, the deck-tennis quoit, the beach ball, the trees, and, of course, the turquoise water. And in this sense Hartman has conveyed the pool's essential dimensions: the screen of forsythia at one end; the wide, unfussy concrete patio; the lustrous, Steinway-black trunk of a maple tree behind two white chaises (mattresses long gone); the blue mosaic; the hedges and deck chairs and vines.

There were swings there that either Hartman has deliberately left out, or has suggested so subtly I'm not sure whether I'm imagining them or not. Sometimes I see them. Sometimes I don't.

The advent of a swimming pool was one of those occurrences that stood out so distinctly from the general blur of family chronology that it was used forever after as a marker. Before the pool. After the pool went in.

The introduction of a swimming pool to our family's life was a happy event. But its construction was a departure from the way things had always been. As a result it had the kind of impact on our family that is more usually the result of tragedy: an old house is torn down; an accident befalls a carefree young woman at a New Year's Eve party; an unexpected diagnosis.

Before the pool. After the pool went in. It was a line in the order of our history. At least, that's what I told Blake when (in that box of white light) he wanted to know why the pool was so important to me.

So I said okay. You asked.

I said, I know it's a swimming pool. I said, I realize it's a symbol of privilege. I said, I understand that, with the possible exception of golf, it would be difficult for me to choose an element from my past more steeped in the affluence of the bourgeoisie. But, I said to Blake (and I knew this was going to be an uphill battle), if you put all that aside and think of the swimming pool as an abrupt intervention in the history of our family, it was like (and Blake's face slipped into doubtful blankness before I finished the sentence) the difference between B.C. and A.D.

So I further explained: Before the pool was a darker world— more shaded and overgrown. And this wasn't necessarily bad. There was a civility, so my mother occasionally noted, to an age that didn't encourage teenagers to lie in the sun on a beach towel on a chaise slathered in coconut oil without speaking to a living soul for hours on end.

Before the pool there was an old garage (with a coal bin) and a sandbox under a maple tree in the back of our house. There was a cedar hedge. There was enough (sloping) grass for a (slightly tilted) game of catch. Before the pool, when relatives visited us in summertime, we sat with them on the veranda at the front of the house. We ate cherries.

My father's frugality had given no hint that something as miraculous as a swimming pool could be in our future. But somehow, when exactly that proved to be the case, I wasn't surprised. Or, to be more accurate: I wasn't surprised to be surprised. I had just become a teenager. Surprise was generally in the air.

After the pool went in, we didn't sit on the front veranda anymore. For some reason we never ate as many cherries. We no longer packed up the car in summertime and drove out to Burlington Beach and parked across the railroad tracks from the dunes. We no longer had picnics in the sand, looking out to the silver glint of Lake Ontario and the pale-blue emptiness of summer.

10

It was Blake who came up with the name. Not me. I didn't know what to call it. I probably wouldn't have called it anything. It was just what we did that December. If he phoned my cell, and it was often the middle of the night when he did, I'd come downstairs to his bedroom and stand beside his bed, and he'd kind of hang from my shoulders. Not all of his weight. Just enough to alleviate some of the pain. He'd lean against me, which I suppose was where the ladder idea came from. He'd shift his balance from one leg to the other. For some reason that helped. And so, on the positive side, that's something. I had what most fathers of grown sons don't: those long, long hugs.

Whether it was Faloney at fault or Patterson didn't matter. The cogent point is this: Faloney threw the ball one way and Patterson cut the other. And the crowd—particularly the crowd at my level and field position—saw all this before they did. What then happened made being sent to my room for sneaking off to a football game a small price to pay. It was a glorious Hamilton moment.

It wasn't all that unusual in those days for an eleven-year-old to be unaccounted for throughout an entire weekend afternoon. As far as my parents were concerned, I could have been with my friends in the woods on the side of the mountain. I could have been playing touch football up at the reservoir. I could have been somewhere on my bike. I'd left clues that might have pointed toward any of these activities. These weren't lies so much as a network of false impressions. This seemed to work.

I'd made my way to the east end of Hamilton by bus. By myself. My parents had no idea that I was sitting in the north stands of Civic Stadium on that fall afternoon, a witness to something amazing.

It was the third quarter. Hamilton was not playing particularly well, and a querulous anxiety was settling in among the fans. I'd thought this would be an easy notch in our belt toward the Grey Cup, but Ottawa was proving troublesome. But then, out of the rubble of a few scrappy through-the-middle rushes, a Tiger-Cats advance began to unfold in front of (and about thirty rows of seats down from) my seven-dollar ticket.

Second down.

Wide receiver Hal Patterson was running a down-and-across pattern that called for Hamilton's quarterback, Bernie Faloney, to throw the ball before Patterson made his move. The ball would be sent to where Patterson was going to be, and not where he was at the moment it left Faloney's reliable throwing arm.

That wasn't in itself unusual. The forward pass in football is largely about predicting the future. Faloney had beautifully precise calculations of distance, arc, and velocities. Those long passes of his (even when he was fading back, even when he was in trouble, even when he was scrambling) were like watching a demonstration of a physics calculation. But this was a much shorter play than those trademark fifty-yarders. It only looked like it was going long.

The key to the play's success was surprise. It was a kind of sleight of hand. Everything that appeared to be the case wasn't the case at all.

Patterson's stride could get everybody thinking one thing when he was thinking something else. And everybody—everybody in Civic Stadium and every single Ottawa player on the churned-up turf of the field—was thinking: long bomb. It would make sense. It could well be that Faloney would pick this moment, in this sequence of downs, to open things up. Certainly Patterson's ferocious speed made it look like that's what was happening. Immediately, you could hear the crowd's excitement rising. This was it. This was it. Ottawa's flared defensive end, Billy Joe Booth, who'd been sidling backwards as Patterson charged toward him, and who was, just now, turning, who was, just now, committing, and who, having seen that hungry, long-ball look in Patterson's lean, determined face, was shifting into overdrive. This was going downtown.

The seats in the north sections were not as cheap as the open wooden bleachers in the end zones, but they were less expensive than the newer concrete boxes on the southern side. The press boxes and the old scoreboard added to the north stand's mystique.

And the fans who sat on the north side for home game after home game—with their Tiger-Cats toques and their noisemakers and their not-to-be-too-closely-inspected Thermoses—were the heart of Steeltown during those blustery, loud fall afternoons.

Everybody in Hamilton understood this. Even the rich people. Those from the more genteel reaches of Hamilton society knew that the city's essence was in the north stands, and they knew that the men with stogies who knew everything there was to know about football and the women in their United Steelworkers wind-breakers with voices that could strip paint were to be given a certain respect. When a drunk (waving merrily to the crowd) was led from the north stands by the police, everybody cheered the drunk.

The fans in the north stands were the fans with the most boom-ing insults and the brassiest trumpets. The north stands were where the greatest cheers of triumph and the most aggrieved shouts of outrage came from. The north stands were Hamilton. And on that October day in 1963, in a home game against their Eastern Conference rivals, the Ottawa Roughriders, when Hal Patterson cut right and Bernie Faloney's pass went left, the north stands were the stands that rose in instant unison.

It was like the huge bellowing of a single voice—as if, in fact, the voice of Hamilton itself was booming over the lids of the coke ovens and the pour-offs of the open hearths, and over the Ladies and Escorts entrances of the old, sour-smelling hotels, and over the Hoover vacuum cleaner sign, and over the patches of front lawn where kids hawked parking for the game, and over the high green wooden fence of Civic Stadium.

"Hal!" the city of Hamilton shouted to Hal Patterson from the scudded grey sky.

It was an immediate blurt of warning. It was a cry that was so rushed and so constricted with emergency there was scarcely a vowel in "Hal." And the great thing was that Patterson seemed to understand immediately what hearing "Hllll!!!!" meant. The north stands weren't going to steer him wrong.

Patterson had already cut. But instead of veering off to his right he continued to accelerate through the spin, adding another one hundred and eighty degrees to his turning, and digging his cleats into the turf for a sudden change of plan. His reversal was more like the firing of pistons than steps. And then he dove, back against his own original momentum, his long arms and legs stretched in a reach of true, All-American magnificence.

Hamilton embraced its American players without complication and with great affection. Of course they were American. They were football players. What did you think they'd be?

There were always a few local heroes on the team—Frank Cosentino, for instance; Ron Howell, for instance—but for the most part the Tiger-Cats were Americans and they seemed to like Hamilton just fine. Not much different from home, they'd say. And we loved them for that. We loved their brush cuts and their broken noses and the shortcuts of their accents. Hamilton was more like Cleveland or Pittsburgh or Buffalo than it was like Ottawa, anyway. We talked more like Americans than people from Toronto did. Or that's what we thought.

And it was hard to imagine anyone more American than Hal Patterson. He was born in Garden City, and he had played baseball, basketball, and football at the University of Kansas. He looked like one of the astronauts in the Mercury program. He was a hero of ours, in Hamilton. The crowd went crazy when he made that catch. We'd been part of the play. We'd been part of that lanky, airborne completion, and in a movie of that time and of that gritty little city that happy cheer would echo and as it echoed it would dim. This was 1963. It was the dawning of a new age.

The trees on Pennsylvania Avenue were as bare as the trees on the side of the escarpment. There was the same autumn chill. Once the leaves were gone, the view from my first bedroom window really did look black and white. A cortège is a solemn procession.

12

If someone in our family said that the fieldstone wall ran the length of the pool, what they meant was it ran the east–west length of the property in which the blue rectangle of chlorinated water sat. The pool, as we understood the word, was contained by forsythia and a rusted fence at the eastern boundary of the property and, to the west, by the cabana and behind the cabana a more antique chain-link covered in the summer with a tangle of wild grape and morning glory. The pool itself—the actual volume of water—held the centre. It wasn't quite a grotto. But it was not without its romance.

I never longed for a pool. Not in the way I longed for a Scalextric slot-car set or a Raleigh three-speed bicycle. I might as well have longed for a rocket ship. If our father wasn't going to pay for a radio in our car the likelihood of a pool in our garden seemed remote. We knew a few people who had a pool, but only a few, and they were distinguished from us by a characteristic of which we were not entirely envious: they were rich.

This was something I said to Blake (as he sipped his ice water, as he gave me that baleful look from his raised hospital bed). Look, I said.

Of course, I understood that compared to the overwhelming majority of people who were living on planet Earth, indeed, compared to the majority of people who ever had lived on planet Earth, we were rich as lords. Our refrigerator was always full. Not only that, the upright freezer in my parents' basement was always full: of hamburger patties on cookie sheets, of gallon cartons of ice cream from Stoney Creek Dairy, of frozen steaks and rump roasts from the quarter-cow my parents bought from a farmer who was a patient of my father's. And then I rattled this list off to Blake, using the fingers of my right hand to number my points: no war, no famine, lots of jobs, vaccines, a relatively benign and largely protective social order. Which is when I started to run out of fingers. Good schools. Cheap gas. Health care. We watered the garden, took long, hot showers, filled our swimming pool, and even flushed our (three) toilets with potable, fluoridated water. We had television. We had baseball gloves. Who needed to be rich?

My father was suspicious of the class above his: they drank too much, they smoked too much. They showed up at church once a year, on Christmas Eve. I was equally suspicious.

Cool was cool. Square was square. Mick Jagger wore slacks and a sweatshirt when the Rolling Stones first appeared on Ed Sullivan. This was the great dividing line. And it was clear to us—meaning it was clear to every kid in every house in the neighbourhood that you can see in John Hartman's painting—what side of the border the rich (with their Bermuda shorts, with their knee socks) were on.

This was a moment too brief to be remembered with any seriousness in the histories of those postwar years. I granted Blake that. But it was true, and actually kind of miraculous when you think of it. There was a time when the (white, North American) middle class didn't want to be anything else. We didn't expect private swimming pools.

But there it so suddenly was: the summer I turned fourteen. At the back of our garden, surrounded by newly poured concrete. You can't miss it in the painting. That's the blue. That's exactly how it looked.

In the painting it's the pool's deep end that's visible. You can't see the corner in the shallow end from which I took my first dive—the first dive, in fact, that anyone took in that pool. The red and white and blue shirt my wife gave me for my sixtieth birthday obscures that part of the pool. Same with the other side. You can't see where I got out at the pool's corner steps the day John Hartman came. That was the last time I ever swam there.

13

So, to be perfectly accurate, there were three friends with me the first time I took LSD. But the way I tell the story—the way I told it to Blake at that dinner table—focuses on only one of them. This was a matter of editing more than anything. I doubt my other two friends would object. It's probably the way they tell it, too. In their recollections, I'm probably in their backgrounds as much as they are in mine.

When someone disappears that's all it is: a nothing, an absence, a splash in the sea that nobody notices. "About suffering they were never wrong,/ The Old Masters." (W. H. Auden. "Musée des Beaux Arts." Introduction to Modern English Literature. Tuesdays and Thursdays. Professor Lindheim. The Larkin Building. No prerequisites.)

It was possible in that pre-internet period of my young adulthood to lose track of people: we graduated, we travelled, we went back to school, we took jobs, we got married, we joined ashrams, we moved. Maybe we died. Perhaps we became heroin addicts. Perhaps we found God. Maybe we'd been in a car accident and we'd been in a coma for decades. Or maybe we just became old enough and comfortable enough to prefer remaining out of touch to being a disappointment. Because this was an often unremarked-upon characteristic of the kind of people who lived in the kind of neighbourhood—brick homes, mature trees—you can see over my shoulders. They would never be quite so good at anything as they were at being young.

Decades later and completely out of the blue, my father asked me, "What ever happened to your friend?"

That was all the identification I needed.

"I don't know, " I replied. "He's disappeared."

"Off the face of the earth?"

"So it seems."

We met at school in Hamilton the autumn before the pool was built. It was on the football field at the reservoir. It was the beginning of a school year. That's why there were some unfamiliar faces.

Touch. Two-handed.

He'd transferred to our school from somewhere, although he never spoke about where that somewhere was.

There are two things I remember about that day. And one was how clear that autumn was. You could feel the last of summer in the sun.

And I remember this:

I'd made a nice catch. That's what we used to say. "Nice. Catch." It was a high compliment.

The only thing more important than being able to make nice catches was being able to run. And after my nice catch, the goal line was about twenty yards of open field away.

He was moving faster than I was, but the angle of his approach was such that I thought I could twist my shoulders and upper body away from his outstretched hands. I continued straight down the sideline.

The impact was just below my knees. Solid. Unhesitant. Fast and thorough.

There were technical distinctions I could have made between a tackle and a two-handed tag. It would have been possible to argue that because two hands had not been simultaneously slapped on my back the ball was still in play. But even though I was uninjured (not even winded), there was something so final about my landing that everything stopped. It was obvious to everybody on the field that I wasn't going to get up and keep going.

He was on his feet. He was holding out his hand to help me to mine.

"No tackling" (shouted furiously) was a time-honoured protest in our games. But it was usually a complaint about being pushed or tripped. Never in my experience had it been about a flying, touch-down-saving, no-doubt-about-it tackle.

"Ho-ly," someone said.

He pulled me up to me feet, and when we were at eye level (the perfect position for shouting "No tackling") I realized I wasn't going to have the chance. He was laughing.

"Spectacular," he said. "You have to admit. We were spectacular."

He was almost a teenager when I first met him, and either he had a big head or there was something about the animation of his features that made me think his face was bigger than it was. He was unusual-looking. When I first knew him—after my pride had recovered from our introduction on the football field and we became friends—I worried that he might grow up to be quite homely.

In this I was entirely wrong. He went through puberty with all the hesitation of a runaway freight train, and as he did his features aligned themselves into an approximate resemblance of Mick Jagger. This was at a moment in history when few resemblances could have been more advantageous to a young man.

If I look back solely on the amount of time we spent together there's no explanation for the closeness of the friendship. He didn't stick around for very long—not that he stayed anywhere for long. His parents divorced. The remnants of his family drifted to corners of the continent that were sufficiently distant from each other to make staying in touch difficult. Which was probably the point.

But we remained friends. We both liked writing letters.

He was more untethered than anyone I knew. Neither of his parents seemed interested in guiding him through his teenage years. And so he found his own way—an unorthodox curriculum that included rooms in various communal households, several long-skirted (usually older) girlfriends, enrolment in a number of non-traditional high school programs, and ("How is this possible?" my traditional father would ask) a lot of travel.

The letters arrived from Calcutta and Kabul and Machu Picchu. They were usually ten or twenty onion-skin pages thick and the free-form scrawl was distinctive if not always legible. Once, in a letter from Tangier, there was a small blob of sticky brown stuff Scotch-taped in the middle of a sentence, immediately after a parenthetical instruction: "(Eat this before continuing.)" I was stoned for three days.

"Your friend certainly gets around," my father said as he sorted through the mail at the kitchen table and tossed another blue air-mail envelope onto my placemat.

What intrigued my father was that my friend (despite incomplete school terms and unfulfilled prerequisites) was charting a college degree through the backwaters of experimental, interdisciplinary undergraduate programs while I still had two more years of traditional high school to get through before university.

My father's own education had been as ordered and sequential as an education could be. He wasn't critical of my friend's lack of orthodoxy so much as astonished by it.

My friend's long hair, Moroccan shoulder bag, and avidity for psychedelic drugs did nothing to disguise how likeable he was. He was charming. And this was a characteristic he put to full use. His good manners, bohemian flair, and white skin worked brilliantly with university registrars in the late 1960s.

My father was confident that there was an order to how you do things. Like get an education, for instance. He had predicted that my friend's decision to skip a term of high school to travel to India would be disastrous. By way of admitting he'd been wrong about this, he would occasionally ask if my friend had finished graduate school yet. Was my friend teaching somewhere? Princeton, perhaps?

My friend represented a departure from the norm, which may have been why my father occasionally asked after him. I don't remember my father inquiring after any other of my friends with the same interest. In fact, I don't remember his asking after any other friend at all. My friend was treated like a visiting emissary from a world my father had been reading about in *Time* magazine. Here, on my father's doorstep—in bell bottoms; with really long hair; wearing a full-length denim coat; having no apparent schedule or means of support—was a hippie. So my father was curious. In my father's world, there weren't a whole lot of departures from the norm.

"Tell me about it," my mother would say.

14

The English-born artist Robert Whale painted Hamilton from the escarpment in 1853 from much the same elevation as Hartman. But there's nothing in Whale's carefully composed scene (a log cabin, foreground; a few blocks of stone row-houses, background) that suggests anything as baronial as the fieldstone wall that ran the length of the pool. The wall must have been built later, when settlement in Hamilton had reached a level of general affluence sufficient for the well-to-do to want things to look older than they really were.

The neighbourhood, so we understood, had once been partly the estate of the Allen family—remnants of which were two falling-down carriage houses and (in a cottage down the street) the last surviving descendent: old lady Allen. The fieldstone had an ancient greyness that Robert Whale would certainly have painted had it been there. But it wasn't. That wall came later—the work of a hired stonemason, and not that of a settler clearing a field.

My birth is the line between the first fifty years of that wall's existence (dignified; vertical) and the less confident inclination of its second fifty. It was leaning alarmingly downhill by the time we sold my parents' property.

The mass of the escarpment loomed behind that wall. The mountain's limestone ridges and boulders, its trunk-sized roots, its cliffs and its creek beds pushed on the neighbourhood's flower beds and limestone garden walls and fieldstone foundations with an unyielding force. The great declining gravity of the Niagara Escarpment leaned into Hamilton as steadily as time. And you can feel that in the painting. You really can.

15

Dreams of flying are not uncommon. In my case, they start with calamity. I am riding my bicycle furiously, trying to escape lunatic murderers.

I go over the mountain brow. That's a Hamilton expression. Mountain brow.

The scaffolding I am climbing (in order to see an important Tiger-Cats football game) collapses.

There is no guardrail on an observation deck overlooking Niagara Falls and my parents reach out to grab me just as I realize too late that the floor is tilting and I am wearing my hard-soled Sunday shoes.

The swing breaks in the high, weightless moment between up and down.

Nothing was ever so unexpected.

16

The pool was built the year of "Doo Wah Diddy Diddy" and "The Little Old Lady from Pasadena." In the painting the cerulean blue of the deep end rises behind my neck like a collar for Elvis.

The water is flecked with a few drifting leaves that never would have been visible when my father was in his prime of pool vacuuming—a period of pool husbandry that lasted for almost half a century. I don't think I possess a clearer memory of him than when he was vacuuming. I picture him somewhere between sixty and seventy. As I am now. In his swim trunks and old sunhat. His routine of pool maintenance became slower and a little more wobbly over time, but it continued until the year before his death.

Beyond the pool is the city where I grew up. And beyond Hamilton, Canada, is the Ontario landscape and the lake that surrounds the grid of the city.

A red brick house is toward the left, about a third of the way from the bottom of the painting. You can see the window of the room where the hospital bed was set up for my mother.

Long before that, the same room was called the playroom. Sixty years before. This was when an artist might have used a mesh of soft gold in a portrait of my mother. There was nothing grey about her in those days. There were young children. There was a rocking horse at that window.

17

There is a summer for which I am often nostalgic. But I'm not sure it was one summer. There is a period—roughly from the time I was fifteen to twenty-one—when my summers are easily confused with one another. There were various summer jobs. There were different books and movies and records. There were girlfriends, and there were any number of evenings and summer days when all we did was get high and laugh and do what we had to do to avoid pregnancy. There was, generally speaking, comfort and security and, compared with much of the rest of the country and most of the rest of the world, staggering affluence. And the swimming pool that you see in the painting was the centre of all those summers. The recurrent setting makes them seem a single season.

For instance, there was the late-summer heat wave when my mother invited the residents of the home for wayward girls to come for a swim. That wasn't what the home was actually called. Even then. But a home for wayward girls was what my father called it—using the almost imperceptible inflection in his voice that signalled that he knew he was employing an anachronism. It was hard to tell whether he intended to satirize the generations who used a term so loaded with presumption or the sensitivities of those who no longer did.

The residence was overseen by one of the organizations for which my mother volunteered. The weather had been blazing for a week. Next to hellish, blazing was the word my mother used most frequently to describe Hamilton summers. And a week of blazing temperatures was enough for my mother. She said: Those girls will perish in this heat.

She asked if I wouldn't mind helping when a dozen young women came over to spend the afternoon in their bathing suits up at the pool. I told my mother that I thought I could probably make room in my busy schedule.

But I'm not sure if the wayward girl (off-shoulder, leopard skin–patterned two piece) who asked me to show her to the bathroom (in the dark, cool basement of the empty house) happened the same summer I was working at the steel company, which was just before I went to university, and if that summer was the summer when I first took LSD. Was that the summer I read *Justine*? Or was that another year entirely? It's hard for me to say. I'm not very good at keeping things in order. I'm particularly bad at keeping the sequence of memories straight. My mother was the same way. "Oh, God. Don't ask me," she'd say when a question arose about how long ago something had happened. "I count on my fingers."

My summers appear a continuum because things changed so imperceptibly up at the pool. The same towels and bathing suits were there from one year to the next. The same Coppertone and board games and chlorine-testing kit. The same (my mother's) Rex Stout and Ellery Queen and (my) *Complete Short Stories of Ernest Hemingway*. And my parents were always there, in the cabana, on those thick Hamilton summer evenings, having drinks with their friends, Jane and George . . .

These details get mixed up now, although I don't suppose that matters anymore. There's hardly anyone to correct me. My parents had a community of neighbours and fellow Junior Leaguers and Medical Arts doctors and Melrose United Church members and Thistle Club curlers and Art Gallery volunteers and Hospital Auxiliary and Ancaster golfers and Players' Guild goers and (in my father's case) childhood friends who came over (this was the wording that was always used despite of how small a percentage of the visit was spent in the pool) for a swim.

My father had grown up in Hamilton. He'd never lived anywhere else—except (during the years of his medical education) at the University of Toronto, Columbia, and the Mayo Clinic. "Min-nes-o-ta," my mother would always say, as if her exaggerated separation of syllables would more fully convey how far away Minnesota was. And how cold the winters were. And how American America was. And how much fun she and my father had being newlyweds in a basement apartment in Rochester. According to my calculations, this is where I was conceived.

This—my father's brief escape from Hamilton to Min-nes-o-ta—was a recurrent subject with my mother. It became more recurrent the older she got. The history of my father's side of the family was sprinkled with attempts to escape it. A great-aunt (Grace) went off to Paris to be an artist just after the First World War. A great-uncle (Ed) went to Japan. But according to my mother, these attempts at freedom were rare—because Hamilton always reached out like a character in a Henry James novel to pull any eccentricity back into its stately orbit.

All told, there must have been about twenty couples who comprised my parents' circle, although my sister tells me that in their heyday they sent out two hundred Christmas cards. My parents' friends were all close to one another in age, family size, race, education, and income level. The men were mostly doctors or dentists or lawyers or engineers or businessmen. And their wives were wives: meaning they were wives, mothers, household managers, tutors, social hostesses, drivers, volunteers. Of the twenty or so couples my parents might have invited round for a swim, I'll tell you about Jane and George.

Not their real names. But not because I am protecting their identities. Their real names have a resonance with me—but that's because I knew them. I'm going to use names that will be more helpful to a reader. I'll call them by the names of movie stars they reminded me of. She looked like Jane Russell, and he bore a kind of haggard resemblance to George Sanders.

Jane and George were the upper reaches of Hamilton's upper middle class. At least I thought so. They were a glamorous couple compared to my parents—a point my mother openly conceded. "I can't compete with Jane in that department," my mother often said, but not so often that I ever really knew to what department she was referring. On warm evenings Jane usually brought something long and flowing and layered in lavender froth to change into when she got out of the water. "A pain warrr," my mother explained. My mother had learned her French in Grand Falls, Newfoundland, where she grew up. In order to deflect attention from her terrible pronunciation, she pretended it was worse than it really was. Champagnee, with a hard g. Quick for quiche. Hors d'oeuvres rhymed with whore's blue days.

George smoked some exotic brand of cigarettes. Pall Malls, I think. No filter. He was a tall, broad-shouldered man, not given to the polite, cheerful enthusiasm with which most adults treated children. If we were coming up for a swim on a hot evening and

encouraged by my mother to step into the cabana and say something polite to the adults about what/how we were doing (at school,
on holidays, on summer jobs) George listened with the level
expression of a skeptical judge.

My parents had changed into something summery and relaxed
for the evening. (My father was not above the white belts and
tapered sports shirts of the day.) But George often came directly
from the Crown attorney's office. He cut a figure of raffish elegance
in his dark-blue suit with the collar of his white shirt undone and
his tie partly unfurled as a gesture to the casual nature of a pool-
side gathering. He didn't say no when my father offered to go down
to the house and freshen the drinks.

And now we come to the reason I've chosen Jane and George.
After all, there were other friends. They were all there in the
middle distance of my parents' lives—a kind of chorus, all mostly
gone now. But George stands out—a bit like the bursts of colour
in Hartman's darker rendering of the escarpment. That's because
George once said something that became so identified with the
pool I can't look at the painting in our living room without thinking of his white shirt, loosened tie, and poised Pall Mall.

My parents and their friends were in their forties—healthy,
secure, prosperous. Were they happy? Well, as a matter of fact, I
think they were—more happy than unhappy, anyway.

The popular explanation for this satisfaction is that the
Depression and Second World War were behind them. But this
didn't quite apply to my parents. Both their families were more
inconvenienced by the Depression than devastated by it. Because
of his childhood bout of polio and slightly withered leg, my father
never enlisted. The aftermath of the Depression and the War for
them was not so much the triumph of industrial production and
the subsequent explosion of consumerism. The lesson of the

1930s and 1940s for my parents was that broken things get fixed. The good guys win. And I do not think it is possible to overestimate the impact of this belief. I think it explains a lot of things that were good about the middle class in those days, and a lot of things that were selfish, and ignorant, and reprehensible. When I was growing up, things were better than they were before. Obviously. This was a trend we expected to continue. And as a result, I think it's fair to say that my parents' quiet happiness on the evening I am describing had something to do with their belief that, all in all, they were in a good place to be. They knew perfectly well that there were peaks and valleys of civilizations of which they had no part. But in the broad strokes of the long and mostly miserable history of the human race there had not been many luckier moments and better places on earth to be white, educated, and alive than ordinary old postwar Hamilton, Ontario, Canada: the economy humming, ice cubes tinkling, science advancing, the pool filter gurgling, democracy spreading, the season turning, the tray of Triscuits and crabmeat being passed.

This was a cause of concern to Blake. He lay in a hospital's blank light while I described to him what the painting brought to mind, and he wondered about people who were so consistently wrong about being the good guys. Was it fair that we had so much and others so little? Well, no. But we imagined that unfairness was being corrected. Was environmental catastrophe not predicted then? Well, yes. But progress always comes with a cost.

None of this washed with Blake. The world was on fire. The drowned children of refugees were washing up on beaches. Corporations were acting like monsters in horror movies. Idiots were in power. Islands were disappearing. Who would care, he asked me: that the languorous setting of that perfect summer evening was the pool at its best. The sky was a dusky rose.

The trees were motionless maps of darkness. The golden lights from distant windows could be glimpsed through the surrounding branches. The reflections of the first stars in the blank surface of the water were like an illustration in an old English book of fairy tales.

"But listen," I said to Blake. "This is why I'm telling you. This is what happened."

My parents were entertaining Jane and George in the cabana that evening. My father had refreshed the drinks.

There was a lull in the conversation. The view through the screens was poised in almost-tropical beauty. This unhurried pause of appreciation continued, as if everyone present had agreed to observe a few moments of silence.

There were a few last cicadas—even at that hour. The summer heat had not yet surrendered entirely. The air was still, and it glistened with humidity. There was the scent of mock orange from a neighbour's garden. The shadows in the surrounding trees turned mauve. George Sanders was smoking. His wife, Jane Russell, was radiant in a lavender peignoir.

George swirled the ice cubes in his Chivas.

He looked out to the trees, to the sky.

He considered the unruffled surface of the water.

There were crickets. There was a sliver of a moon. The view, framed by the cabana's screens, looked like an old illustration of midsummer's eve. Which, as a matter of fact, is what it was. This happened to be the evening of the summer solstice. Late sixties, I think.

George sipped his whisky. He continued to consider a view that, with some cropping, could have been a Pre-Raphaelite painting: a knight's secret lagoon hidden in a glen of trees. Dusk.

"Well," George said. A pause was always included when my mother told the story. "The days will be getting shorter now."

This remark became one my mother quoted (for the rest of her life, actually) as evidence of the undercurrent of gloom she believed to be resident in certain deep pools of Hamilton society. No summer solstice passes without somebody in our family quoting George, and, of course, the funny thing is he was right. They are getting shorter now. But as I say: I'm not quite sure what summer that was. They get mixed up. Was that the summer I read *The Electric Kool-Aid Acid Test*? Or was it *For Whom the Bell Tolls*? And I wonder: Was that the summer I played golf with my father for the only time in my life? These are the kinds of questions this painting raises.

18

She is a nurse, although her uniform is a little less uniform-like and a little darker than what nurses usually wear. She was born in India but has lived in Canada, in Toronto, for many years. So she is Canadian. Let's get that straight. She has a beautiful face that is often described as handsome because her narrow features are so strong. She has straight, greying hair; a trim, neatly compact figure; and excellent posture.

This part is shot in black and white. And she is lit with the shadowy, in-between lighting of Josef von Sternberg.

It's not her voice that's otherworldly. Quite the contrary. Her voice is so unhurried and solemn it carries the whole sad weight of the world in the text she speaks. Directly to camera. She says:

Interior. Donny's house. Night.

She says: There is a landing just inside the back door. Useful for boots and fall jackets. This is November.

The stairs go down to the basement. And up to the kitchen. The basement (dry, partly finished) has a furnace room and ample storage space. This must be where Donny's father keeps the gun.

A narrow set of stairs go from the kitchen to the second floor. There are three bedrooms off the hallway, plus a three-piece bathroom. This is before ensuites became common.

Donny's mother is asleep in the master bedroom. Donny has his own room. So does his older sister. She has a ticket to Petula Clark (O'Keefe Centre, Toronto) stuck in the side of the mirror on her dresser.

The small window of the master bedroom looks over a neat but slightly barren front garden.

The house (orange brick; three-storey) is conveniently located, steps away from the local bus route. The walking trails of the Niagara Escarpment are close at hand in this gracious, desirable neighbourhood.

Donny's father comes up the narrow stairs from the kitchen. He has a management position with Fuller Brush. He is an active member of Central Presbyterian. Once he starts he doesn't stop.

He flicks on the lights in Donny's room. The brightness explodes. And when his son sits up in bed, he shoots him. Then his daughter. Then his wife. The second two shots are immediately fatal. The first was not. Donny crawls to the landing. That's where his father shoots him again.

He uses the front, central staircase to go back down. He sits at the dining-room table in the well-lit ground floor. The house is ideal for a small family. Across the street somewhere a dog is barking. It's a friendly, family-oriented neighbourhood with excellent local schools. Then he goes back upstairs and shoots himself.

There is no explanation for any of this. Ever. The house goes unsold for a long time.

three

The northwest corner of the pool is just below my right shoulder, off the stretched linen's bottom edge. There were three steps down into the shallow end. It became one of my favourite places to read.

Because reading was what the pool was for. Beyond swimming, I mean. And sunbathing. And, every now and then, when the stars aligned, sex.

No electrical things (radios, record players, and once, unsuccessfully for the moon landing, a portable television set) ever worked more than briefly up at the pool. There were periods of enthusiasm for board games and cards. Exercise fads came and went. But reading was a constant.

Inside the cabana was for reading the *New York Times* and the copies of *The New Yorker* that my parents' more worldly and well-read friends left behind when they came for a swim on Sundays. At first the dense pages of text, especially in *The New Yorker*, seemed above my pay-grade. But eventually I got the hang of them. I often didn't know enough about politics for the political stories to make much sense to me. Frequently, I'd never heard of the artists or tycoons they profiled. But I knew enough about sports to get the sports stories—those long, unhurried, fantastically discursive sports stories.

The Sunday *New York Times* had an astonishing number of pages to keep out of even the slightest summer breeze. *The New Yorker's* pages had a glare in the summer sun. For these reasons my memory of reading David Halberstam, Roger Angell, and Herbert Warren Wind for the first time is of reading them in the calm and civilized shade of the cabana.

But the place to read a book was outside, at the northwest corner of the pool. My feet were sometimes on the first, sometimes on the second underwater step. I'd sit there, with the book between my knees. I got a few nasty sunburns on my ankles.

"Back in the saddle, I see," my father said when, after a couple of days of rain, he was vacuuming around where I had resumed my position, at the corner of the shallow end with *The Doors of Perception* or *The Teachings of Don Juan* or *On the Road*. Was the Hemingway summer the same summer as *The Alexandria Quartet*? And was that before or after the summer I came up for a swim early one June morning, and then went straight back down to the house to get my father? I get those summers mixed up now.

I didn't know what to call it when I told my father what I'd seen. "There's a mess up at the pool," I said. It was an odd announcement to make, and that's probably why my father put down his coffee and his newspaper and came immediately.

It was where I always sat, at the corner of the shallow end, with my feet on the underwater steps. The two oblong red smudges were in exactly that position.

It was like a dog had been sick or something. The smudges were too thick to have dried and they were partly on the concrete, partly on the mosaic lip of the steps into the water.

"Somebody's had a baby," my father said calmly, and then went to phone the police.

They searched the neighbourhood you can see in the painting. They looked through the woods (there, to the left of my head) for the rest of the day.

2

I could see that Blake was suspicious of the whole thing. I'd be suspicious, too. That's what I told him in the hospital one day. I admitted that it would be a coincidence if that boy under those clanging stairs was who I thought he was. But there it was. A coincidence. It didn't have to mean anything. But that didn't mean it didn't happen. Of all the Hamilton schoolkids who would have known the doggerel about Evelyn Dick, it was Donny who I first heard recite it. Under those back stairs at Earl Kitchener. On that grey playground. It was a coincidence a writer might be tempted to invent.

But it wasn't coincidence that Blake objected to. As a general rule. He was quite okay with coincidences. A lot of the movies he watched were full of them.

We didn't talk much about the horror movies he liked. Probably Blake would have been embarrassed by my ignorance of obscure Italian directors and American cult classics. But I'd always liked horror movies as a kid. I'd even considered myself something of an aficionado. Fright Night. Channel 7. Buffalo.

A shared appreciation is one of those connections a parent can have with a child. It's a kind of shorthand. It's a signal that, once in place, acknowledges: this is one of the things that relate us. I always found movies good for this. Caroline and I had *Edward Scissorhands*. Blake and I had Withnail.

Blake came up to our room while we were watching the British movie *Withnail and I* one evening. In the late nineties, probably. We'd stuck stubbornly with Betamax until ours was stolen. So *Withnail and I* would have been VHS. Blake must have been nine or so, and he arrived at the top of the stairs (a position with an unobstructed view of the television screen) just at the beginning of the scene in which Withnail, played so brilliantly by Richard E. Grant, is stumbling around, knee-deep in a trout stream, trying to shoot fish with an antique shotgun. I can picture Blake's pyjamas.

There are three reasons I keep this moment in mind. And the first is that it was some kind of transition for Blake. If he started up those stairs as a little boy who couldn't sleep (and it wouldn't have been the first time) he reached the top with a calm absence of crisis. We were watching something that looked interesting. Perhaps he'd join us. We suggested to him that maybe he was a little young for *Withnail and I*, but without saying anything he dismissed what he sensed were our pro forma objections to his not being in bed. He moved slowly into the room. Slowly he sat down. His attention was fixed on the screen. His eyes widened. His smile spread. Withnail floundered in the water, blasting great, useless, double-barrelled explosions of spray.

Next reason: the scene itself. And why it sticks in my mind is that Blake got it, even though there is nothing particularly funny about a man blasting a shotgun into the creek in which he is standing. But this is exactly what Withnail would do, which is what makes the scene so funny. Blake had shown the same capacity with some of his quirkier friends. He got them. He'd always liked oddballs.

And lastly: that expression of Blake's. Some people have a beautiful laugh. Others, a radiant smile. And not that there was anything wrong with his laughter or his grin. But what he had that was quintessentially Blake was an expression that gradually expanded across his face. It went from interest, to amusement, to astonished delight with steady graduation. When he was with a story, he was really with it. It's what made him a good editor. At least, that's my guess.

3

He was in remission by the fall. He'd regained some weight. "Cautiously optimistic" is what I told John Hartman when we were standing in my parents' driveway and he asked. It was my standard answer, mostly because it was true. I said we sometimes forgot he was sick, which wasn't. There is part of a parent that never forgets when a child is sick. It's situated in the pit of the stomach, in my experience.

An offer on the Glenfern property had been accepted, and much of the stuff in my parents' house had gone by then—to auction and to junk dealers. By the autumn day you can see in Hartman's painting, the outside of the house looked much as it always had. Inside, though, things were different—different from the way things had been for sixty years.

There were remnants. The piano, for instance. You can't give away a piano these days.

My mother's decorative plates on her decorative plate rail.

Nobody wanted the sofa. But even on its own, adrift in the middle of a mostly empty room, it managed to remind us of what things had been like when 25 Glenfern Avenue had been an active address: when there had been bridge nights and cocktail parties. When there had been Christmas Eves. And Junior League teas. And wedding anniversaries. Or my father's retirement party.

The character of the living room had faded so slowly it felt as if its diminishment would continue, perhaps forever. Which was stupid, obviously. There was a closing date.

If you think of the Hartman painting as being a portrait of a writer staring thoughtfully into the future, it's important to remember that he's gazing thoughtfully into a future about which he is entirely wrong. The one and only consistent lesson of being a magazine writer was this: not much is ever what you expect. Nothing is going to happen the way the subject of Hartman's painting wants it to happen. Nothing is going to be the way he thinks it should be.

When the worst happens, the only useful lesson is the knowledge that it can: time can actually run out, sadness can actually prevail, a world can actually end. But I didn't know there was sadness like that then, of course. Sadness like that wasn't part of my background.

Blake occasionally drew pictures of himself in this period—partly doodles, partly sketches for the graphic novel he was thinking about doing. He used the cartoon convention of simple crosses for eyes to convey being sick.

The day I met John Hartman for our tour of Hamilton was, I think, a Saturday—a not-quite-warm, occasionally sunny Saturday afternoon in early October. That was a few years ago now, and that's something else I notice about his painting of that day. When you are in a picture, the time that has passed since it was painted becomes an element of what the picture is.

My only plan for being John Hartman's guide that day was to follow the example of my father. He wasn't a big talker, my father. He kept some impressively lengthy silences. I've recently been wondering if I inherited them—if the hours I spend in my office aren't more like my father's unhurried gaps of Hamilton speechlessness than I'd suspected.

But my father was almost chatty in his last years—at least he was when he was being driven to appointments and therapists and diagnostic tests around the city. His Hamilton came to him in whatever order the city did as we drove through it—with no distinction between civic history and family lore. "That's where Rocco Perri's wife was blown up," he'd say, pointing out an alley we were passing—the site of an infamous gangland slaying during Hamilton's roaring, rum-running twenties. (See *The Whisky King* by Trevor Cole.) My father always claimed he heard the explosion of the car bomb from his Duke Street bedroom. And then, as if continuing to the next item on the same list, he'd say: "And that's where Aunt Grace taught art. Before she went to Paris."

So that's what I thought I'd do.

"That's where the famous murderess Evelyn Dick buried her husband's torso," I'd say, pointing (generally, vaguely) to the escarpment. And then, as if the ten or twelve blocks of synchronized traffic lights along Main Street were an ellipsis in the same sentence, I'd eventually conclude, "And that's where my grandfather's haberdasher was."

I asked Hartman if he wanted to start our tour by heading out to the east end, to see the remains of Hamilton's steel industry. No doubt I used the term "rust belt." You hear it as much these days as you'd have heard "lunch-bucket town" when I was growing up. We were standing in the driveway at the time. I had the car keys in my hand.

Hartman is a fit, pleasant looking sixty-something-year-old. He has a friendly, down-to-earth Ontario twang in his voice and a genial courteous manner. But somewhere in the distance of his patience I could hear that this was something that we had already discussed. Evidently, I'd forgotten. "Evidently" being one of those words my father liked to use—and that I use from time to time, mostly as way of remembering my father.

"I can always drive around the city on my own," Hartman told me. He spoke with the determined clarity with which people repeat things. "Let's just walk. Around here. I want the royal tour. Of your Hamilton." He put a little weight on "your."

I have a busy memory. There are dentist appointments and grocery lists and dry cleaning pick-ups that have no evidence of their existence anywhere other than in my mind. That's because I am unreasonably confident about the reliability of my powers of recall—a holdover, I think, from my multiple deadline days. A functioning memory was one of the few job requirements for a freelance magazine writer. So I take a certain professional pride in remembering things. But sometimes I get them wrong. Evidently.

It wasn't surprising to me that Hartman would be interested in doing a portrait of Hamilton. He is well known for his big, aerial, map-like views of cities. He studied art in Hamilton at McMaster University in the early 1970s.

It even made sense that he would ask me to be a guide. I'm no expert on Hamilton history or politics. But I have some local knowledge—most of which was passed down to me by my father. In fact, in the years following my father's death, during my visits to my mother, I'd discovered that remembering my father usually involved remembering what he had to say about Hamilton.

Do you know: there is an actual pain that comes with missing someone. It's a stabbing sensation—although more hollow than sharp. Perhaps it's more like the memory of a wound than anything. Sometimes, when I was visiting my mother and I missed my father (his decency, his gentleness) I'd just go drive around.

I am certain that John Hartman is correct. He says he told me exactly what he was thinking of doing, and there is no reason to doubt him. He is methodical in his work. Informing me that he was planning a portrait of me with Hamilton in the background, or a portrait of Hamilton with me in the foreground, would have been step one in a carefully planned process. Somehow this information passed me by.

Hartman's painting of me went unsold at the gallery show at which I saw it for the first time. It was a bit of a shock. The painting, I mean. Not the fact that nobody bought it. My wife said she wasn't surprised. "None taken," I replied.

There is something (and this is exactly the right word) unsettling about unexpectedly coming across a giant portrait of yourself in an art gallery. It was a confusing moment. Three days later, the painting and two art installers were in our downtown Toronto house.

It's poised between being a picture of a city behind me and a portrait of me in front of a city. It's as if the painting exists on two planes—both of them in focus and both of them insistent on equal attention. The painting's refusal to make up its mind gives it an ambiguity that I've come to appreciate.

I'm not sure how much the painting looks like me. I don't have a very accurate sense of what I look like—not as I get older, anyway. But what I do know is that the painting feels right. And that's the best I can do in attesting to its accuracy as a portrait. I can tell you that it feels like one of those candid shots that surprise you, not always pleasantly. It's not at all how you picture yourself. But you sense somehow that a certain truth has been captured.

The painting has a tone that is familiar to me. It looks like it has the same memories I do.

Death can take away details that once upon a time we imagined we could never possibly lose. How frustrated Blake used to get sometimes at his mother's unassailable logic. How loping his running was. How he laughed when he trapped a queen with two pawns. How he looked when I picked him up to take him to emergency that first time and I asked what was wrong and he said he didn't know. How his voice sounded coming from a hospital gurney that was being wheeled beyond where I was allowed to go when he said: "So long, old man."

Seize the day, people say. Unhelpfully. Days end, whether seized or not.

There are family resemblances that disappear as soon as a parent, a child, and a grandchild can no longer be seen together, arms in a trio of hands and shoulders. These resemblances—of movement, gesture, inflection—are rarely captured in birthday photos or graduation snaps. And they are the things that vanish. This was the lesson I was starting to learn in the October afternoon you can see in Hartman's painting. Things vanish. I was in my sixties by the time I came to know—really know—this to be true. The ghost of my mother would be sure to point out: that's how lucky I'd been.

4

The palliative care nurse speaks directly to camera. Her solemnity gives her a presence that there, in the bright white light of the fourteenth floor of Princess Margaret Hospital, seems surreal. It's as if she's not really there—as if she's a hologram, like Princess Leia in *Star Wars*. She is dignified, almost regal. She has straight, greying hair and a narrow, handsome face. Her manner and her voice are calm. Her words sound more like a prayer than a prognosis.

She says: William Macfarlane.

She says: Presently 99 days following 10/10 matched sibling donor transplant for mixed phenotype acute leukemia (MPAL) that occurred on a background of relapsed negative B-cell acute lymphoblastic leukemia with MLL (rearrangement of the MLL gene), diagnosed in April of 2014.

She says: The *Pietà* that is now in St. Peter's was completed between 1498 and 1499. It is known for the beauty of Michelangelo's carving and for the mystery of Mary's youth. She looks like a young mother. But her son, taking the place of the baby once in her lap, is a grown man.

She says: The recent, November 24, 2017, bone marrow aspirate and biopsy is indicating relapse of the MPAL with 30 percent blasts on the bone marrow biopsy sample. The transplant team have indicated that if the percentage of blasts can be reduced to 5 percent then consideration would be given for Donor Leukocyte Infusion (DLI).

She says: Commissioned by the French Cardinal Jean de Bilhères. Carrara marble. 1.74 by 1.95 metres.

She says: A young mother. Strong and bold and unfrightened by the future. This was 1988. A young mother who prided herself on walking to the hospital. It was a grey, ordinary November day. She walked across the St. George campus and along College Street and down University Avenue to the hospital for his birth.

5

I'd been returning regularly to Hamilton for a few years by the time the city came up in conversation with John Hartman at the Nicholas Metivier Gallery. The purpose of these visits was for me to help my mother—or, as she put it, "your aged mother." She'd been describing herself this way since she was younger than I am now. But by the second decade of the twenty-first century she really was aged—alone in the house she'd lived in for sixty years, declining our suggestions that we hire somebody to help her look after the place.

In the five years between my father's death and my mother's I spent more time in my parents' house than I had in years. My sister lives in Hamilton, and she and her family kept by far the closest eye. But I tried to help, at least a bit. Sometimes I'd drive in for dinner and stay overnight, sleeping in my old bedroom in the basement, and trying (rarely with any success) to beat the traffic back to Toronto early the next morning. On other occasions—mostly in the warmer weather—I'd come in from Toronto, usually on the bus, and stay for three or four days.

This was a worrisome period—by which I mean, there was a lot of worrying about Blake going on. Not always, of course. Not constantly. But the future you can see me looking toward in Hartman's painting is what I mostly wondered about, and that future is where I am now. What I didn't know then, I know, and the interim is what the painting is about—at least, that's what it has come to be about for me. That's what I see.

After an early dinner in Hamilton (when the weather was okay and while my mother worked on a crossword puzzle in the TV room at the back of her house) I'd smoke a joint on the front steps of the veranda. This was in the slightly confusing, not-exactly-legal-yet period of cannabis legislation in Canada, and so I had to be discreet. I liked to imagine old Mrs. Mills, who lived next door when I was little, calling the police.

And then, at a brisk, healthful pace, I'd walk the streets that are hidden under the canopy of autumn leaves that can be seen in Hartman's painting.

I found a snapshot of me on those streets that I like. It was in one of the photo albums that I flipped through while we were dismantling my parents' house, and because I don't often like pictures of me, I unstuck it from its position in the album to get it copied, and then, of course, in the confusion that attends death and the dispersal of chattel, it disappeared. I keep thinking it will turn up.

I was eight or nine when the picture was taken. I was slender in the same way Blake was slender when he was the same age. (We both got pudgy around eleven. And then, around fourteen, un-pudgy.) The picture of the young, slender me is black and white and a little blurry, but what I liked about it is how obviously happy I am. I'm brimming with the fun of going wherever I was going.

Janice and I have a few photographs of Caroline and Blake that capture the same kind of moment—one of them is a snapshot that Caroline keeps on a mantel in the bedroom of her Brooklyn apartment: the two of them splashing in the shallows of a sandy narrows behind a cottage in Georgian Bay we rented. Blake was a gleeful moment or two away from realizing that he could swim. It used to be a hard picture to look at and not smile. "Not a care in the world," my mother always said of that snap.

I won't claim to have encountered a ghost of my young self on my evening walks in Hamilton. The cannabis wasn't that strong. But what I did meet, now and then, under that roof of mixed forest, was a clear memory of being that boy in that photograph: the feel of the sidewalk under my Keds, the bounce of energy in my step, and my ("entitled" Blake would have correctly pointed out) confidence that happiness would not be whisked away. Not by anyone. Such was the enduring stability of Ontario's postwar middle class that in the half century since that photograph of slender me was taken almost nothing had changed on the sidewalks and up the driveways and across the front gardens and under the verandas and over the hedges of the streets I'd known when I was young. It was like going back in time. That was my discovery.

6

It was Donny. I'm sure it was him. I remember exactly when the memory came to me. I remember sitting in our living room in Toronto, looking at that painting and remembering that playground and (out of the blue) thinking: Can that be right? Really? Was it really Donny?

It was hazy, that memory. Iron-oxide-and-zinc hazy. It was on the very edge of being lost in the mists of time.

I have the feeling that he wasn't going to Earl Kitchener anymore. I'm not sure why I think that, but part of the confusion about the memory has to do with my sense that he was, by then, going to another school, with different holidays. He's come back to Earl Kitchener for recess. Just for fun. Just to visit. His very presence on the playground is slightly against the rules, and this gives him a certain panache. The collar of Donny's windbreaker is turned up. A sharp look, I think.

We stand around him, shoulder overlapping shoulder. As if what Donny is telling us is a pilfered cigarette, or a jackknife, or a dirty picture.

Mr. Parsons' flapping beige raincoat. You. Boys.

Donny rushes the last line, and everybody laughs, and the circle dissolves into the dun of tag and skipping and catch. And that's it.

But it wasn't because it was Donny that I remember this scene. That wasn't why it stayed with me as it did. What later happened to Donny was so outside of any sequence we could have predicted that there was no reason (at least no reason pertaining to the gunshots in his future) for me to remember that moment on the playground.

Donny was a little older, and that was enough of a difference between us to ensure that we were only nodding acquaintances. He wasn't someone to whom I gave much thought one way or the other. I doubt he knew my name. There must be hundreds of other gatherings and playground games and secret clusters that I've forgotten. Why, then, does that circle of boys in fall jackets under those clanging stairs stand out?

So I had to think about it. I really did. I sat in our living room, trying to recall what details of that scene I could. Perhaps one memory would lead to another. And I suppose that's what happened because gradually I realized I knew why that grey schoolyard came to mind when I sat and looked at that painting.

It's because I was embarrassed. That's all. It's funny how these things stay with you. I was embarrassed because I didn't get the joke. *You cut off his arms, You cut off his legs. You cut off his head. How could you? Mrs. Dick?*

I didn't know what was so funny.

November. 1963. Afternoon recess. Grey light.

7

I will tell you as I told Blake, and I will tell you without fear of being contradicted by the most travelled enthusiasts of the game, that the Hamilton Golf and Country Club is a beautiful course. It's beautiful in the unspectacular, old-fashioned, gently rolling way that southern Ontario can be beautiful on a cloudless blue morning.

I had the good sense to establish this context when I told Blake and Caroline the golf story the first time. I realized that an important element would be missing if they didn't know that it was a truly lovely old course. Because that's what saved me. Everything was so beautiful.

I needed to provide some background to Blake and Caroline for the story to work. And the background was this: that old course was especially magnificent on the summer morning when my father nodded toward the Men's tee and said to his son, "Lay on, MacDuff." It was seven-thirty.

I suppose the story was trotted out every couple of years or so, and eventually I began to guess that Blake knew exactly what I was describing. Not the golf, so much. He didn't play golf. None of us played golf. But by the time Blake was in his twenties I began to get the impression that he could accurately picture what a beautiful old golf course looked like on an exquisite summer day in southern Ontario when you were on acid. I always described my father on the third green, scorecard in hand, pencil poised, peering at me with a puzzled expression when, for the third time, I couldn't remember what I'd just shot. For the life of me, I couldn't. And it was always at this point in the story that Blake's eyes were at their widest and most gleefully attentive. Because he could picture his grandfather, and he could picture me, and he could easily imagine how every hole would be a saga of event if you happened to be on LSD. The number of times I hit the ball must have always seemed entirely inconsequential. Blake could see that. And that was when he started to laugh. I remember that. It was as if that steadily expanding expression had become more than his face could contain. It was one of those really special things: a story that a child enjoys listening to and a parent enjoys telling. They don't always coincide, I've found. Once in a blue moon. Before we all end up dead and buried.

At the course in Ancaster there are big, mature maples and oaks in its generous roughs. A soft-shouldered creek meanders across six of its fairways. Its broader water hazards, fed by mossy culverts and tucked into groves and hollows, come upon the unwary by surprise, as water hazards often do.

Harry Colt, the designer of the course, had strong views about what worked in a golf course and what didn't. He disliked greens that could not be seen from any reasonable lie on the fairway. He objected to sand traps and ponds and stands of trees that bore no relationship to the land's natural state. He liked fairways carved into glens so that it looked like a river or a glacier had left their lush, shadowed paths. He liked golf's generous, sky-high bigness, but he also liked the slow reveal of a tight, two-stroke angle. A turn in the course of play was, he felt, "an accurate test of the game"— meaning that it separated those who had the distance and accuracy and nerve to go over a dangerous point of rough from those who more prudently played around it.

Colt disapproved of a player ever having to retrace steps on a course. Golf was a progression that unfolded invariably—from one to eighteen, in order. A course has its own pace and rhythms within the unchanging sequence of play. For players to be forced to walk back, even a few steps, through a chapter that had already ended in order to get to the next tee was a flaw. No doubt there were situations of terrain and water when it couldn't be avoided by even the most artful of course designers. But going back the way you came in order to go the way you needed to go was almost invariably a failure of design, in Colt's view.

Reversal ran counter to the sport's relentless regard for the future. It was like life: deep in our instinct for survival is our hope for the shot we are about to make. Colt believed that's what a golf course was: the ordered, but constantly surprising geography of what we are about to do. He liked things that beckoned.

The old trestle footbridge and the flat wooden cross-overs along the creek were among the few obviously man-made impositions on the gracious, rustic scenery. The landscape itself gave the impression that it had emerged, only slightly refined, from the natural world, sand traps and all. The little wooden-shingled rain shelters looked like the mountain huts in which you might expect to find a holy man studying the *I Ching*. And while Ancaster may not be world-famous, it has always been highly regarded. Edward, the Prince of Wales, played it once. So did Nicklaus, Trevino, Crenshaw. And so did the great Bobby Jones.

Jones was probably the greatest amateur player of all time. He won thirteen major championships in the 1920s. He was a co-designer of the Masters course at Augusta National. Herbert Wind once wrote, "Golf without Jones would be like France without Paris—leaderless, lightless, and lonely."

And I made a point of mentioning this to Blake and Caroline, and to anyone else at the dinner table at which I picture myself telling the story of the only time I ever played golf with my father, because it was an important point to make. Not only was the golf course beautiful. It was serious—serious meaning that it existed in the realm of courses that good players want to play. These were eighteen challenging holes—challenging enough that a golfer as great as Bobby Jones found them to be no walk in the park. As a matter of fact, the course my father and I were approaching that morning (our golf shoes clattering across the parking lot between the locker rooms and the pro shop) was serious enough to be the site of one of the greatest tournament rounds ever played.

Sipping discreetly but by no means surreptitiously from a flask in his golf bag, J. Douglas Edgar played an almost flawless four rounds of golf that weekend. This was (almost to the day) fifty years before the summer morning my father and I showed up to play.

The LSD was the best I ever had. I was surprised I hit the ball, frankly.

It must have been some kind of survival instinct. Because I can remember that in the car, sitting beside my father while he drove us out to the golf club early that summer morning, I consciously reviewed my golf lessons. Step by step. Instruction by instruction. It seemed the only sensible thing to do. Fortunately, as per usual in those days, my father was not inclined to talk.

As the reality of the first tee presented itself, I could see that there was risk of real embarrassment here. For a moment I was afraid I wouldn't be able to balance the ball on the tee.

I stepped back to take a couple of practice swings. And this was when something unexpected happened.

My review of my golf lessons in the car had been quite detailed. I was surprised I could recall them with such clarity. But even more surprising: my practice swings. My body seemed to under-stand something that had previously escaped me. The torque of hips, the stationary shoulders, the unmoving head. I could feel how it all worked, and this was (somehow) inextricably bound up with how beautiful everything was. As I say, it was very good LSD.

As a teacher, J. Douglas Edgar resisted breaking the golf stroke down into sequential elements. A little mystically, he called his teaching method "the gateway." He believed that a swing was such an organically fluid movement it was as if everything in it happened at the same time.

Mine were not astonishing shots. They were not particularly long. They were not particularly high. But they were decent. And I remember feeling proud of myself as I marched off down the first fairway with my father. And he was right. It was a beautiful morning. "Not bad," he said. "What do you say to ten cents a hole?"

8

When our house in Toronto was first built (1887) the room at the front of the ground floor was called the parlour. Sometimes the front parlour, although there was no other.

When it was the parlour it was the most formal of all the rooms in the three-storey, semi-detached house. The house was owned by a Toronto contractor named William McBean. He constructed a number of nearly identical houses in the late-nineteenth century throughout the old core of the city. Nearly identical houses being his line of business.

It wasn't that McBean lacked imagination. It's just that he was familiar with the economic constraints that came to bear on a particular swath of the city of Toronto's growing population. These were the hard-working citizens—neither rich nor poor—who bestowed on Toronto the industrious and modest civic personality that prevailed throughout most of the twentieth century.

Their homes embodied the practical, frugal nature of who they were. Shopkeepers. Teachers. Factory workers. Merchants. Clerks. That being the case, there weren't a lot of variations on the theme. Variety added costs, and McBean houses were priced for respectable members of Toronto's middle class—of which William McBean himself was a proud, by-his-bootstraps member.

And let it be said: No moss grew on William McBean. Our house was his model home—a residence he lived in with his family but that had a purpose beyond the strictly domestic. Across the room from the wall with the oil painting I looked at every morning was McBean's hearth.

The front parlour is where, fire lit, McBean smokes his pipe and reads the Toronto *Evening Telegram* when he gets home from work every day. It's an unchanging ritual—which is an illusion that interiors help create. The insides of homes don't change very quickly—the newspaper and pipe where McBean left them, the city's dusk reflected on the wallpaper, the same as ever. I remember this myself: our mornings of packing school lunchboxes, of waving to Caroline and Blake from the front door, of picking up groceries for dinner, of insisting on piano practice, of helping with homework, of lying in bed after making love and hoping (sleepily, happily) that we didn't wake the children. There was a time when our world seemed to go on and on. It actually did feel like it would last forever and now, looking back, it feels like it lasted no time at all.

McBean can show you the hearth (handsomely tiled) and the armchair he prefers. And here (as if the idea of showing his own home to a prospective client is only now occurring to him) he points the way down the narrow but neatly proportioned hall (note the wainscotting) and through this panelled door: his wife is feeding their two cherubic children in the kitchen. A happy scene. Ample cupboard space, as you observe.

William McBean was a good salesman.

McBean owned a number of lots nearby, none of them very wide, all within an easy walk of the shops of Harbord, College, and Spadina.

The garden is the size of a postage stamp. That's sometimes how people described it. And that's how my mother always did. She often invited us to Hamilton for a visit, especially during the summer. She was a great believer in children running around—something she didn't think ours did often enough in the notorious slums of downtown Toronto.

"But they're playing in the garden right now," I'd say on the phone on a Saturday morning when the weather was starting to get hot and her invitations became more insistent.

"But they can't run around there, can they? It's the size of a postage stamp."

So, yes. The back garden is small. McBean wouldn't have denied it. It wasn't a backyard that took very long for our children to outgrow.

Going through the gate to the sidewalk on their own was a big step. Like almost everything else to do with being a parent, it came earlier than I expected.

I still use the geography of Caroline's and Blake's steadily expanding Toronto as a way of ordering my memories of their growing up. "Only to the corner store" was something we shouted every now and then from whatever we were doing. No longer contained by the postage stamp of our back garden, they got to know the alley behind our house quite well when there was catch or hide-go-seek. Then, the neighbouring streets became places they were allowed, apparently, to go. By the time they were ten or so, they managed the reach of the subway.

I like to think my father felt what I did when I took our kids to the airport for their first big trip somewhere. But I don't know. I was his eldest child on my way to Europe for the first time. He was, I think, apprehensive. As was I. Did they have their passports? Did they have their wallets? Did they have their phones? But I wonder if my father would single out waving goodbye at security as a particularly proud moment. Because I would. They were on their way somewhere. I could see they'd manage.

There were periods in our family's history when the space that had been McBean's front parlour and that was now our never-quite-sorted-out living room was not without activity. The piano was there and that meant that for a few years the living room was useful for at least half an hour a day.

Otherwise, its activity was intermittent. It's where everybody shouts Happy New Year. It's where the four of us always had our Christmas mornings. The living room was where the kids would make forts with the cushions sometimes, when their friends or cousins were over.

But that room could have been the subject for an article for an interior design magazine, and my wife could tell you why. It was off the beaten track. The natural currents of our daily comings and goings in that house passed it by. My wife, who is a designer, hates rooms that have no purpose.

That could have been my article's opening sentence. And there was a time when there were half a dozen magazines in Toronto that might have paid fifteen hundred dollars for an amusing but informative piece about what to do with a room that could go for days without anyone stepping into it.

There were a few magazine writers in more or less the same situation I was—friends mostly, knocking around Toronto editorial offices, pinched by mortgages and household expenses. We were looked down upon by creative writers. Such, at least, was our belief. They wrote about sex and death. We'd write about throw pillows if the per-word fee was enough.

We shared a few editors. We shared a few restaurants and bars where we met editors. Sometimes it seemed we shared the same narrator: the calmly bemused, curiously well-informed, comfortably well-off but by-no-means wealthy representative of everyone born white and middle class between 1948 and 1964 in North America. When we bought a house, we wrote about residential architecture. When we had children, we wrote about childcare and education. When our children went away, we wrote about houses that were too big.

A feature article about the challenge of an under-utilized interior would have fit right in—probably in a lifestyle monthly, but there were even general interest magazines that might have run it. The easy humour of the article would make it clear to readers that my wife's and my particular solution to the problem of the un-used room is not an answer for everyone.

That's because there's a band set up in our living room. It gets together once a week. The gear is always there.

Two keyboards, a drum kit, various amps and mic stands and guitars. There's a PA, with two monitors, one of them perched on the piano we inherited from my wife's parents. There are patch cords everywhere. There are tambourines and maracas and a couple of acoustic guitars. And there's usually one or two not-quite-empty wine glasses left from last week's practice. Blake sat in on drums sometimes.

One of the least endearing characteristics of my generation is its assumption that every other generation is interested in what we are doing, and so, naturally, I wrote a few articles and columns about the band for various newspapers and magazines. There were a few girls in Blake's class in grade eight who thought it was pretty cool that Blake's picture was in *GQ*. George Clooney was on the cover.

Rock and roll. Some classic R&B. A bit of a miracle for me, actually. It's the only band I've ever been in.

Someone I'd worked with a lot over the years suggested we start one. He'd often been my editor. We are friends. We'd known one another for a quarter of a century. I thought I knew John pretty well. But I didn't see this coming. At first, I wasn't sure I'd heard him correctly. Aside from the occasional "O Canada," I never sang anything. My guitar playing was what might generously be called campfire strumming.

All the reasons not to start a band presented themselves immediately to me. We'd be terrible. We'd look ridiculous. We would conform (with dreary precision) to one of the most predictable stereotypes of the aging male. Not a motorcycle. Not a sportscar. Worse. Electric guitars we didn't know how to play and amplifiers with lots of switches we didn't understand. I thought: "Mustang Sally." And my heart sank.

When someone you know well, like a lot, and for whom you have the greatest professional respect makes a suggestion that you think is crazy, conversation can be difficult. What do you say when what you want to say is: Are you out of your mind? But John continued, untroubled by my silence.

He told me that when he was a boy he used to listen to the radio in his bedroom in Toronto. He could pick up stations at night—sometimes from great distances.

He'd adjust the dial with the care of a safe-cracker. He narrowed in on the slender, silvery beams of 50,000-watt clear channels. They came from Buffalo or Cleveland or Cincinnati or who knows where in the south, carrying Louis Jordan or Elvis out on the airwaves through the cold and frictionless air. John's pop-music centre of gravity was earlier than mine and more authentically American, I felt. He told me that when he first heard Buddy Holly on his little transistor (and these are his exact words) his head practically exploded with how good it was.

He stayed up for hours that night trying to find another station, somewhere on the airwaves, playing "That'll Be the Day."

He said he wanted to have that music back in his life. That was all. He didn't think we'd look cool on stage. He didn't think women would be impressed. "Quite the opposite, probably," he said. He just wanted to play songs like the songs he heard when he was a boy and the nights were clear. This was his only reason for wanting to start a band. It seemed like a good one to me.

9

There was one afternoon in the spring of 2017 when I was able to study Blake's face for a long time without his noticing. I was peeling carrots. He was home from the hospital for a while and he was sitting at the back of the house, looking out the window. He was micro-dosing LSD at the time, which I didn't know. It was our daughter who provided this detail a few months later. She knew exactly what afternoon I was talking about when I mentioned how intent Blake seemed to be on the view that day.

I paid attention to Blake's voice when he was sick. When he was calling from the hospital, or when he was on his couch in his apartment in our basement watching *Star Trek*, or *The Twilight Zone*, or *Paths of Glory*, or *Reservoir Dogs* and I came to his door with tacos from Kensington Market or Banh Mi Boys sandwiches from Queen Street, I'd listen. If I heard confidence in his voice I felt better. Even if I thought he'd put it there for my benefit, I felt better.

However, when it came to assessing how he was really feeling, Blake's voice was a less reliable gauge than his face, and the only reason I didn't search his features more closely (looking for optimism, looking for health) was because he always caught me. "Stop doing that," he'd say. He hated people looking concerned.

But on this occasion, I stood at the kitchen counter, peeling carrots and looking at my son without interruption. Blake was intent on whatever he was looking at through those large back windows. It was a grey day, but the light's good back there. This had not always been the case.

The rears of the houses McBean built were evidence of his careful attention to cost. They were solidly utilitarian in aspect. The backsides of McBean homes are not among the triumphs of Victorian residential architecture.

They were plain brick walls, a few begrudged windows, and (over time, increasingly insecure) a wooden shed. In relation to the main body of the house, McBean's mudrooms were often more leaning-against than attached-to. Ours certainly was. I wasn't sure what held it up. There were a few holes in the floor you had to watch for.

It stayed this way for quite a while after we moved in. In fact, the mudroom stayed that way for years. But eventually (around the time Caroline was entering grade nine) it became apparent that the back shed was going to collapse if we didn't do something.

One thing led to another. As things do with old houses. Now large windows look over the postage-stamp garden.

Blake often sat there when he was home from the hospital. Sometimes he read. Sometimes he played guitar. And sometimes he just looked out those windows.

The view could hardly be more prosaic: the insulbrick siding of the house across the alley, the garage-roof shingles, the old fences, the fire escapes. But I figured Blake was looking intently at what he couldn't look at when he was stuck in a hospital room. He was looking at the light.

Our new windows meant that the light came from the east, the south, and the west, angled by northern latitude, fretted by branches, filtered by cloud. It was a luxury, that light. Sometimes when I was driving Blake home from the hospital he stuck his head out of the car window (just like Withnail, actually) as if the air was something he wanted to gobble up.

Blake was a handsome young man—and you don't have to take my word for it. Once, the four of us were on our way to some event at a downtown hotel. It was a wedding or a graduation or something—one of those important semi-formal functions that occupy a family during its middle history. Blake, I remember, was looking particularly flash—in a skinny, vintage-store black suit. His dark curls completed the young Bob Dylan look he had going when he was twenty or so. He had a coolness that I actually envied—envied in the retroactive sense of wishing I'd had such an asset when I was his age. Because I noticed (from the vantage of invisibility) that the young women we passed on the sidewalk as we approached that downtown hotel gave him a look.

We kidded him about looking cool even when he was sick. And it was true. Illness sculpted his features—never more so than on the afternoon when he learned that the stem cell transplant had failed. (The bone marrow aspirate and biopsy indicating relapse of the MPAL with 30 percent blasts on the bone marrow biopsy sample.) I'd come in the back door of our house a few moments after he'd got the phone call from the hospital. He'd collapsed in the front hallway. His mother had caught him, and they'd crumpled to the floor together. He was lying across her lap as pale as Christ in Mary's arms.

He had a sharply defined face. His shoulders were square. I remember standing at the kitchen counter peeling carrots that afternoon, and thinking how handsome my son looked. And I thought: I'll always remember this. It sounds sentimental, I know, but it was actually more an observation than anything. I'll remember how beautiful everything was. The light was too clear to forget.

10

Slightly to the left of my head in the painting there is a swath of black as wide and thick as a knife-full of peanut butter. If you look at it on its own—if you focus on the heavy dash sufficiently to separate it from the neighbourhood in which I grew up—it's inexplicable.

Literalists would say there was no such object. There was no long glob of iron oxide (crested with phthalo turquoise) on Aberdeen Avenue, in the city of Hamilton, in the province of Ontario, in the country of Canada. But there it is, more or less level with my right eye—about the speed-blurred shape of a comic-book bullet on its way to my head. And the strange thing is, I said to Blake, it looks like it belongs.

Hartman's painting is textured with this kind of thing: colours that seem too bright, shapes too undefined, knife-fulls of chroma too thick to exist in the natural world. But there they are. These explosions contrast with the more common greens and browns of a mixed deciduous background. These colours stand out the way angels stand out in medieval triptychs.

But listen, I said. Here's what's odd.

One morning, while sitting in our living room, while drinking a coffee, while looking at Hartman's painting, I remembered that there really was something black at the corner of Queen and Aberdeen. It could be charred ivory crested with turquoise. I'd almost forgotten. It used to give me bad dreams.

Now and then it was my father. More usually it was my mother who had to come hurrying down the hall in the middle of the night.

The house at the bottom of Spruceside, across Aberdeen near Queen, was an address to be avoided. Shortcuts through the property were not advised. The house (shadowy, outlined with verdigris) was set back, in the middle of an overgrown and tangled lot. It was occupied by a lady who was very old. Maybe dead.

We were sure that the old lady's stubborn invisibility was evidence of supernatural power. Or madness. Or both. And our conviction had entirely to do with her house. It was exactly the architecture of a good many of the houses in the horror movies we were allowed to watch on Friday nights.

This was a weekly ritual, instituted when I was nine years old. There were usually four or five of us—neighbourhood friends, approximately the same age, boys. Operating on the theory, I suppose, that at least they knew where we were and what we were doing, our parents agreed that we could take turns meeting in one another's houses for Fright Night.

It was always a double-header. So there was a certain amount of walking home along Mapleside, or Spruceside, or Hillcrest, or Glenfern at 2:30 in the morning. After seeing *Psycho* and *Night of the Living Dead*.

For a while I had a morning paper route. This presented other opportunities to scare myself. If I saw the bundles of newspapers on the park bench at the bottom of Spruceside when I was on my way home after *House on Haunted Hill* and *The Pit and the Pendulum*, I'd do my papers a couple of hours before the first signs of dawn. There was never anyone around.

The TV listings were consulted every week to see what horror movies we had in store. The listings were published on Tuesdays, and they had their own little spark of interest, especially when read on a dark street while delivering the papers they came in. They were written in a matter-of-fact present tense: "An eccentric millionaire dares his invited guests to spend a weekend in an old house"; "Newlyweds discover that a curse still haunts a family estate"; "A mysterious Count purchases the property next to a girls' boarding school."

I was a boy. One of millions in North America at that time. I was, therefore, exactly the demographic at which most horror movies were aimed. I was a pinpoint of marketing. Candelabras, cobblestone, horse-drawn carriages and girls in nightgowns were components of this vernacular.

We looked down our noses at movies with modern settings. These were usually the second feature of a Friday Fright Night. Suburbs like suburbs we knew. Neighbourhoods like ours. They were the horror movies that Blake would come to consider classics. The invasion of a pleasantly affluent middle class by zombies, by aliens, by body-snatchers, by some mutating force of malevolent science was a recurrent theme. These movies were almost always about monsters that lurked beyond the tidy streets and well-kept neighbourhoods of nice, ordinary people like us. The horror movies I liked were more picturesque.

The house at the bottom of Spruceside near Queen and Aberdeen was well back from the sidewalk. It was surrounded by a high and (as per the traditional requirements of a haunted house) not entirely upright iron fence. It could have been a long glob of iron oxide crested with phthalo turquoise.

I called it the Spooky Place when I was very young, and for a few years the name stuck. Even my parents called it that, as if they were pronouncing the name of an estate owned by a well-known local family with an unfortunate last name. It was torn down in the 1960s—veranda, chimney, gables, widow's walk, iron gates all gone, replaced by a row of perfectly pleasant, perfectly tidy two-storey townhouses.

Urban geography is not difficult to erase. Here, in Toronto, when a new building goes up, as they do all the time, I often find I can't remember the brick and cornice and stone lintel that were there before. During the autumn of 2017, when we drove back and forth, and walked back and forth, and rode bikes back and forth to the Princess Margaret Hospital, sometimes dropping Blake off, sometimes picking him up, sometimes delivering meals and smoothies and requested hard drives or memory sticks or DVDs or books, there was a four-storey brick building at the corner of College and Huron Streets that we watched disappear over the course of a few weeks. It wasn't anything so special, I suppose. But it was handsome and solid, and the stonework was good. The windows were nicely proportioned. And it was part of the city we used to have. It was just a building on the way to the art gallery that the four of us walked by now and then.

It's the same with paint: a rag and a little linseed oil are usually sufficient to get rid of something. If the paint has dried, fine sandpaper works.

The perfectly pleasant townhouses at the corner of Queen and Aberdeen in Hamilton are the least surprising buildings imaginable. And that's why they always surprised me when we drove in to visit my parents. They are directly across the street from the park bench where I used to pick up my bundle of newspapers. They were never what I was expecting to see when we turned up Spruceside Avenue to Glenfern.

"Now and then" would be a pretty good description of how regular our visits to my parents were, although, when our daughter and our son were young, the frequency of trips increased with the temperature. "You're bad pennies, that's what you are," my mother said when she took their hands and marched—she always said marched—them straight up to the pool before they perished in the heat. That's also what she always said. "Those children will perish in this heat." But even when it really was hot and we were visiting Hamilton frequently, I couldn't get used to those townhouses.

In those days, when we arrived in Hamilton it was always the same. I can picture it exactly. As if the light is still there.

My mother stands up from her weeding. She has the agility of a much younger woman, despite having never to my knowledge attended an exercise class in her life. That will be the frosty Friday were her precise words.

She disdains the aquafit classes many of her friends attend. And not because we have our own pool. She hardly ever swims. I cannot remember when I last saw her in the water.

She smooths her summer dress. She takes her grandson's left hand in her right hand, her granddaughter's right in her left, and together they walk ("the three heroes," my mother turns and says to us as they march upward) through the luminous halo of the summer of, oh I don't know, 1992.

There were three stone steps. Right there. I can point them out in the painting. And there's the old gate to the pool. And even though the turquoise water isn't visible from the bottom of the garden, there's a brightness in the air that makes it clear the pool is there. I don't imagine that has changed.

11

Blake's view from where he sat in the back room of our house in Toronto was eastward through the upper branches of the trees that pop up among the parking spaces toward the backs of the buildings on Spadina Circle. And if you sit there (as I sometimes do now; looking at exactly the view he had) you'll see that the lower portion of what Blake could see was cut off by the foreground of garage roof and wooden fence.

At the ground level there are garbage bins and gates and rusted bicycles and bits of trash and abandoned shopping carts and patched asphalt. But this part of the view is out of sight. And if you knew nothing about Toronto, you could imagine that you are looking out over a park. And because it's a park you can't actually see, it could be an improbably beautiful park in which everything moves in slow motion. Why not?

Perhaps there are ponds and fountains and footpaths obscured by the fences and carport roofs. Perhaps the trees and the sky you can see are the upper reaches of a graceful commons. Maybe cellophane flowers of yellow and green are hidden by our neighbour's sway-backed garage. Perhaps newspaper taxis. I picture the park that isn't really there as a peaceful, vaguely psychedelic scene.

Blake's musical passions were drawn from a canon I knew little about: hip-hop, dub, house, electro-beat. The records in his collection were mostly indie bands and DJs and remixes: Broken Social Scene, Animal Collective, Flying Lotus, Panda Bear, MF Doom, Wu-Tang Clan, Death Grips, Arthur Russell, Actress, Mount Kimbie. He saw Sun Araw in Montreal and said it was one of the most magical concerts he'd ever attended.

But there were other important figures for Blake who were also names I recognized. He was a big fan of the Band, particularly Levon Helm's drumming. He used to kid me about how much I like the Beatles, but he liked them, too. So, like me, he may well have had "Lucy in the Sky with Diamonds" in mind when he looked out our back window. He was on LSD, after all.

Other than overhead wires, of which there are many, the only evidence that what you can see from the rear of our house might not be a Peter Max panorama is the University of Toronto's utility chimney to the east. It's about the height of Godzilla.

But on that afternoon, when I was peeling those carrots and our son was sitting at the back of the house, I was able to look at him for a long time—longer, probably, than any time since the occasions when I'd watch him sleep in a crib. Long enough, anyway, to notice for the first time that his eyes had the same expression as the eyes in the portrait in our living room. The colours—umber, Payne's grey, cobalt, zinc, aquamarine, dioxazine violet, and sienna—combine to more grey than blue. They aren't sad eyes so much as eyes surprised by sadness.

The back of the house couldn't have been a highlight of the tour that McBean gave any of his prospective customers. It was too perfunctory. "And this is the back" is about the most that could be said of the old back of our house. Any benefit that southern exposure might have bestowed on the inhabitants (light, for example) was avoided in McBean's tightly budgeted design. For more than a hundred years the back of the house wasn't anywhere you went unless you had a chore or a bowel movement to attend to. But from the day our new windows were installed, the back of the ground floor became the favourite place to sit.

This left the living room even more at sea than it already was.

12

For the first ten years of the band's existence we practised at a house on the east side of Toronto. It belonged to the writer Alison Gordon. We had to set up around her ex-husband's snooker table.

This was a small price to pay. Alison's basement was pretty much perfect for us. As was Alison.

From the jacket blurb of her mystery novel *The Dead Pull Hitter*, published in 1988: "Alison Gordon is a sportswriter and columnist for the print media, radio, and television. She spent five years covering the Toronto Blue Jays for *The Toronto Star*, the first woman to cover the American League beat." We practised once a week.

There was a television down there, and Alison sometimes turned it on (with the sound off) during our practices. She watched baseball while playing tambourine. She got to be quite good.

Alison was a writer who had stopped writing. This was a deliberate decision, one she didn't talk about, but she hadn't published anything in a magazine or newspaper for a few years. If this troubled her she took care not to show it. She carried on being Alison Gordon.

Every week, we sat with Alison at her kitchen table. Wine, usually. And during these pre-music conversations we sometimes caught a glimpse of how spectacularly her life was populated. She had something of which she was very proud. She had (and the two words that follow these parentheses have to be pronounced as Alison would have pronounced them: with the hint of emphasis that conveys very deliberate understatement) interesting friends.

Alison protested the Vietnam War at Queen's University. She campaigned for Pierre Trudeau at his leadership convention. She worked for CBC Radio in the 1970s. She was a good writer, and could be a very funny one. She wrote droll magazine articles—some for *National Lampoon*. She'd had her share of adventures and love affairs. She could tell you stories. Mostly, chose not to.

Alison got around. Hers is one of the voices singing "Give Peace A Chance" with John Lennon and Yoko Ono in a Montreal hotel room in 1969. She was friendly with *The New Yorker*'s great baseball writer Roger Angell. She went birding with Margaret Atwood.

So that was Alison.

A heart attack. She went ahead (it was an expression of hers) to mix the drinks.

Suddenly and unexpectedly, the band was bereft of Alison. A few months later, once the affairs of her estate wound down and the house was put up for sale, we were also bereft of a place to practise.

Meanwhile, at our house: the renovation of the rear ground floor had thrown our living room into a spiral of aimlessness. The magazine article almost writes itself.

The band practices in the living room every Wednesday. When he was at home and feeling up to it, Blake would sometimes sit in on drums. "I Shall Be Released." "Into the Mystic." At first, the enormous painting of me seemed a little strange. But everybody got used to it quickly enough.

13

Not many people get to consider a portrait of themselves while returning in the evenings from the corner store with a quart of milk. Not many get to sit in front of one for fifteen minutes or so with a mug of coffee in the mornings. And so I can tell you with the confidence of a frequent eyewitness that the long view and the short view of Hartman's painting are different experiences, but that both involve looking at something that's bigger than you expect it to be. The surface area falls about halfway between the size of a framed photograph on a mantel and a billboard on a highway. I'm only slightly smaller than Jacques-Louis David's *Napoleon Crossing the Alps.*

The painting conveys an impression of size. In fact, its size is a good part of what the painting is. And this, in itself, is another of the painting's uncanny accuracies. If I imagine the interior of our living room as the mind of a memoir writer, the size of the unjustifiably enormous portrait of me in the middle of it is probably about right.

The living room has high ceilings. That is our home's grandest feature. Otherwise: it has a structural modesty that even the wildest and most costly renovations of our newest and richest neighbours can't shake. Our living room has dimensions that make a really big and really colourful painting seem even more conspicuous than it is.

The painting in our living room is only about ten feet from the fireplace opposite. You can't back up far enough to make my portrait seem not-huge. No other object in the room occupies as much visual space as that painting. Not the drum kit. Not the guitars. Not the electric keyboards. Not the old piano that was here years before the band moved in.

After his diagnosis, Blake returned to live with us. There's an apartment in our basement—installed years ago at my wife's insistence. In a cold-eyed assessment of our future, she had decided that it was not beyond the realm of possibility that we might retire down there and rent the rest of the house out. And the apartment that Janice designed for our old age turned out to be perfect for Blake in his youth. Acute lymphoblastic leukemia with MLL, diagnosed in April of 2014. He was twenty-five. By then, no one had played the piano in our living room in a while.

The piano's first owner, a bachelor, wore its hammers down to the nubs during the three decades it occupied a sitting room in a small town in rural Ontario. From the day it arrived at our house (the movers were only briefly slowed by the narrow dimensions in which they had to work) the piano seemed to have a particular personality—in part, I think, because I imagined its first owner playing it with such sad, passionate loneliness—Chopin, surely. This quality clung to the piano's varnish the way resonance will accrue to a frequently played guitar. For some reason, I had quite a clear image of the bachelor pianist's sitting room. I pictured flocked wallpaper and his mother's silk lampshades.

My wife's parents acquired it—an upright Steinway—at a country auction for next to nothing and put it through another thirty years of domestic use. And then it came to us, a little the worse for wear and, to be honest, a little too big for our living room.

But it's a good, resonant instrument in an unusually resonant house. "Country Gardens." "Clare de Lune." "Eine kleine Nacht-musik." For a few years we enforced an after-dinner piano practice regimen with Caroline and Blake and there was always something assertive about that piano. It had an insistent clarity. This was especially true when being played by a child who didn't want to be playing it.

The piano is the same varnished black as the trunk of the maple tree that can be seen in Hartman's painting. The tree is between a pool and a garden. And there actually is such a tree. Such a pool. Such a garden. I can vouch for that.

Steinway would be a good name for a paint colour. It's the kind of black that feels as if it has a rich, lustrous brown somewhere in its depths but that, the more closely you look, the more black the black is.

I don't spend a lot of time with family photographs. It's not so much that they make me sad, although they do. It's that I find them frustrating. I always want to know why what's happening in a picture—a picture of two children, let's say, splashing in the sandy shallows behind a rented summer cottage—can't still be happening. Somewhere. Somehow. That light can't vanish completely. Can it? Where does light go? It has to be somewhere. Doesn't it?

Ridiculous questions. But that doesn't seem to stop me from asking them when I see old snapshots, and so, as a general rule, I don't get out the photo albums. But I do wish we had archived family sound. I would like to hear how that ordinary Toronto house sounded on one of those ordinary evenings: an argument about homework, a bath running, a radio (CBC) talking and talking. The same mistake in "Eine kleine Nachtmusik." Over and over.

The old Steinway had been mostly silent after the last of the children's piano lessons. For twelve or thirteen years hardly anyone touched it. Life was going on elsewhere, it seemed during this period: there was high school for Caroline and Blake, there was university, there were travels, there were jobs, there were gigs. We were empty nesters. And then we weren't. And then we were. But when Blake was diagnosed and he packed up the apartment on Bloor Street that he shared with a few musician friends and moved back to live with us while undergoing treatment, he got that piano tuned. Then Blake found a piano teacher who would come every few weeks, depending on how Blake was feeling.

He learned Hank Williams' "I'm So Lonesome I Could Cry." It was a simple arrangement. Blake played it at a slow, measured tempo. I wish I had a recording of it coming up the stairs. My office is on the second floor of our house, over McBean's front parlour. So I was always in a prime listening position. But really there was nowhere you couldn't hear it.

14

When I looked at the dark masses of the trees from the window of the bedroom I had before it became my youngest brother's, I liked to imagine trails of rustlers and the coasts of pirate seas. This sounds, I do realize, like bullshit. But it's actually true. The tumult of leaves and the network of branches were easily transformed into Buffalo Gap or the North Inlet of Ben Gunn's island. This was accomplished with some elementary hallucinating.

I let what I was actually seeing—the dark boughs, the skeletons of branches—go out of focus enough to become other things: sagebrush canyons and secret coves and forest hideaways. At that time of the evening, the view was pretty much in black and white anyway. Which helped with general authenticity. *The Lone Ranger* and *Treasure Island* were television shows we watched in those days. So was *The Adventures of Robin Hood*. Colour was years away.

There was a horse trough on the corner of Queen and Aberdeen until the late 1950s. I actually remember it. It was as big as a bathtub, and cast with iron garlands of vaguely imperial filigree. And the Spooky Place—the turreted, sway-backed, copper-eaved, weather-vaned old house that used to preside so darkly at the corner—was exactly what a traveller would expect to see were he to stop at dusk to let his horse drink at that trough even though the innkeeper had advised him most urgently to get off the road, good sir, by sundown. Fright Night. Channel 7. Buffalo.

I sometimes woke in the middle of the night and, from my bed, looked southward, up to the dark woods. Wasn't it strange, I thought, that when the old, possibly dead lady at the Spooky Place stood at the second-floor bay, above a veranda no paintbrush had touched for decades, pulled back the tattered wisps of curtains and peered toward the darkness of the mountain, she was looking in the same direction I was. Perhaps at the same spot. At the same moment.

The leaves on the trees of the slope of the escarpment looked to me like continents. And that may have been how the old lady thought of them, too. Her continents. And what if she could trace the angle of my vision back to my window and to the red railroad tracks on the grey cotton prairies of my bedspread?

I must have been seven the last time. There was something less than sympathetic in the quick, angry clip of my mother's footsteps down the hall.

She flicked on the lights. "You're too big for this kind of nonsense," she said. Then she turned the lights off. And she was gone, more slowly this time, down the hall.

15

Peter and me. "Peter and I," my mother would say.

Hope and me. "Hope and I," my mother would say.

Graham and me. "Graham and I," my mother would say.

Russ and me. "Russ and I," my mother would say.

Alan and me. "Alan and I," my mother would say.

Bill and me. "Bill and I," my mother would say.

Gilmour and me. "Gilmour and I," my mother would say.

My friends and me. We were sort of a club—largely because there were a few of us and because we undertook building a clubhouse as frequently as we abandoned the idea. We were also kind of a gang. But more like Spanky and Alfalfa than the Jets and the Sharks.

Among other subversive activities, we walked to and from school tossing balls from one sidewalk to another. Sometimes footballs. Sometimes rubber balls. Sometimes baseballs. Some-times old tennis balls.

Even on busy streets this was tolerated by drivers, so long as gaps between vehicles were wide enough and we lofted the balls sufficiently to cause no interference with traffic.

It's an image of perfection that has stayed with me: a scuffed, American League hardball ball thrown perfectly between the hydro lines and telephone wires of my side of Aberdeen, arcing high over the oblivious traffic, then falling between the hydro lines and telephone wires on the other side of the street, and (with a satisfying snap of leather) into Graham's or Russ's or Robbie's or Mitchell's waiting baseball glove.

In the history of the postwar North American middle class, this was near the end of the period when it was understood that throw-ing a ball from sidewalk to sidewalk (or skipping double dutch at curbside, or learning to ride a bicycle, or playing in the big puddle that formed every spring at the corner of Glenfern and Kent) were the kinds of things that went on in a street.

We became more daring when the balls we were throwing were less lethal than an actual baseball. Sometimes too daring. But I was never really frightened by the men who stopped when we clunked their cars with a misfired split-finger tennis ball. They'd pull over with an angry jerk of their steering wheels and leap from their Impalas and Cutlasses, flapping their all-weather coats and holding on to their fedoras. And it's telling, I think, that they didn't frighten me. I wasn't particularly cocky. But there was, somehow, an assurance in the air in those days. It was per-vasive in the textured grid of streets you can see in the painting. It was nothing we acknowledged because it seemed as ordinary as undergrowth—the flat chrome-oxide green of burdock and milk-weed and thistle that grew all over the side of the escarpment.

But, in fact, it was miraculous—as miraculous as colours too bright, shapes too undefined, knife-fulls of chroma too thick to exist in the natural world. And the miracle was this: we believed that no adult would harm us.

Forget the swimming pool. Forget the golf club. Not being afraid was privilege. This was real privilege. We thought no adult could harm us, and as Blake pointed out more than once, that wasn't what Black kids thought. That wasn't what Indigenous kids thought. When men, red-in-the-face and sputtering, marched toward us in their London Fogs and Biltmores, with their car doors ajar, we knew: nothing really bad was going to happen. They wouldn't hit us. They wouldn't kidnap us. They were more funny than anything, although we were always careful to look full of solemn regret. We took them to be on the same querulous frequency as some of the crabby teachers we'd encountered. This was because there were people who had been left a little crazy by the war. That's why they were so bad-tempered. Or so we thought. We accepted occasional outbursts of high-pitched adult anger as part of the general climate of Hamilton. We'd apologize to upset drivers. We'd say we'd be more careful. And that was that. They'd climb back into their Meteors and Parisiennes and drive away. But we didn't say we'd stop throwing balls: over telephone lines, over tree branches, over streets. We wouldn't have been expected to.

These days, were you to ka-thwang the side of a panel truck with a miscalculated long bomb from Faloney to Patterson, you'd probably end up in handcuffs. And this is a related point that I emphasized to Blake about the neighbourhood in the painting—at least as I recall it. There was a framed portrait of a pretty young woman in the hallway of Earl Kitchener Junior Public School. That's why that blue is called Royal. At least, that's what I thought.

She bore a striking resemblance to my mother. It wasn't so many years later that I began to wonder what the Queen of England had to do with a place like Hamilton. But there was a time when, along with schoolmates and teachers and pretty much everybody, really, I believed in the Queen to the extent that I believed in an order over which she reigned, in some kind of partnership (we'd been led to believe), with God. And so, it's important to know this about the brick houses you can see in Hartman's painting. I said to Blake. This was their claim to fame. This was their achievement. Nothing was really going to hurt us on those streets, and this was because there was an order to things. And bad things weren't part of the order. Oh, there were exceptions to this. The Dicks. Donny. A baby buried under a bush on the escarpment that nobody ever found. But they were exactly that: exceptions. We thought. They proved the rule. We thought. They were a retreating darkness.

Prosperity was part of our neighbourhood's order. So was progress. So was comfort. So was health. But that didn't mean we thought those houses, those hedges, those trees were anything special. We just thought they were the way things were supposed to be.

16

It was while John Hartman was at McMaster University in the early 1970s that a professor—the sculptor George Burton Wallace—introduced him to the work of Lucian Freud. I know this because when Hartman and I were walking along the side of the Niagara Escarpment that October afternoon in 2014, I asked him about portrait artists he admired. Freud was the first name he mentioned.

This raised a question. With Blake. And once Blake raised it I couldn't quite shake it. If I didn't know that Hartman was painting a portrait of me, why was I asking him about portrait artists? "Who are the portrait artists you admire?" would be a question a soon-to-be subject would ask of a painter. You'd think. And Lucian Freud is an answer that would give pause to anyone who thinks he is better- and younger-looking than he is. Uh-oh, I might have thought. Lucian Freud would have stuck in my mind.

So I told Blake (skipping his question altogether) that my only point in mentioning Lucian Freud was to make it clear that Hartman had his own connection with Hamilton. It didn't seem at all strange to me that he should want to paint it. He has his own memories of the place. And for a while (until I checked the dates of his art school years) I wondered if the swath of thick, iron-black D. L. Stevenson oil paint like a speeding bullet to my right eye might have been inspired by the shadowy darkness of the Spooky Place. But Hartman was at McMaster several years after the Spooky Place was demolished. The dense, overgrown property couldn't have been anything he was referencing.

Similarly, there's a burst of orange in a yard that looks like fire. But it can't be fire. I don't think anyone on Glenfern Avenue has burned leaves in their back garden in October for fifty years. So, I'm not sure why the orange is there, except that it feels right to me that it is, and that could be because there was a time when everybody had yard fires in autumn. And perhaps that bright D. L. Stevenson light is something that's still there. Somewhere. Those clear blue days were laced with the smell of burning leaves. In the soft brown jacket he wore as a young man, and the old hat he put on when he was working in the yard, my father was holding the hand of his first-born child. I was young, obviously. But now I'm old enough to realize that he was, too. The leaves are alizarin red, sienna, cadmium yellow, umber, and oxide. He was holding me back from the orange fire, and when I tried to tug him closer to the flame, he looked down at me and said, not unkindly: "Do you have bats in your belfry?"

The dozen or so colours Hartman uses add up to the form of the painting, and overall the form is big. I first saw *David Macfarlane, Hamilton* at the Nicholas Metivier Gallery on King Street in Toronto, and even among other sizeable canvases it was bigger than you'd expect.

When I return to our house from a walk to the corner store at night, and if the lights in our living room are on and the drapes open, I can see that neighbours must think we are watching a gigantic flat-screen television—unless their glances rest long enough to notice that the talking head (long grey hair; brightly striped shirt) isn't talking and doesn't ever move.

The head looks as realistic as an image on a Trinitron when seen from the sidewalk at night. But at closer range it is unmistakably a painting. A sable brush can leave a softness between things. A hog's bristle, which is what Hartman prefers, has a more abrupt edge. As a writer, I envy this: the ability to place one colour directly beside another, without segue. Seen up close, the lines on my face—of age, of shadow, of worry—are as blatant as a stage actor's makeup.

17

Real estate agents will tell you that a swimming pool is usually considered a disadvantage when it comes to selling a property. This came as a surprise to me. A pool was a plus for some buyers. A minus for others.

"A wash," is what the agent said.

I'd always imagined the opposite to be true—at least in our family's case. And that's another reason I find Hartman's painting so strangely accurate. The prominence of the swimming pool is quite a precise rendering of just how wrong about things I can be.

Over the years I hadn't really thought very much about what would be involved in selling our parents' house, even though its eventual sale was an ever-increasing possibility as they got older—at least in theory. "Over my dead body," my mother said, which is pretty much what happened. But insofar as I ever did imagine how the Hamilton real estate market would respond to the red ("Arts and Crafts–style") brick house and the sloping ("gracefully proportioned") back garden, it was always the pool that I thought would be the clincher. I pictured an agent revealing it with great drama—as if, astonishingly, an enchanted forest or a secret garden came with the charming four-bedroom house with driveway and mid-efficiency furnace in desirable west-end neighbourhood. I thought people would take one look at the bright, expansive magic of that turquoise and buy the place on the spot. That's how much I knew.

For many, a pool is less an asset and more a calculation of how much it will cost to fill in. All the things that I liked about the pool—its bigness, its oldness, and its unusual, isolated positioning between the backyards of two streets—were not thought to be strong selling points.

"Not particularly," were the agent's exact words.

When I was at university the industry of creative writing classes had not yet fully established itself. This left student literary reviews, quarterlies, and monthly broadsheets as the most likely vessels for publication to which an aspiring writer could turn. Which wasn't a big help. At the college level, literary journals were jealously guarded by fourth-year students in jeans and academic gowns who read Rilke and wrote sestinas. The next rung up—the

small literary magazines available to a more general readership—
were run by the same people, slightly older and without the gowns.
Or so it seemed to me.

I'd written a short story about my summer job at Stelco in
Hamilton and there are only three things about that story I
remember.

1. It was described by everyone who read it as
   "Hemingway-esque."
2. Its title was "Steely Nights in Tiger Town." And the
   reason I remember the title is because I was quite
   proud of it. It was five words long, and yet, in those
   five words you could find: William Burroughs,
   William Blake, Federico Fellini, the Kinks, the
   postwar industrial North American economy and
   professional (Canadian, of course) football. Being
   stoned helped, I will admit.
3. Everybody I sent it to rejected it.

As a result of my inability to break into print there was no easy
way to identify myself at university as someone who hoped to be
a writer. The days of using a college tie for a belt and keeping a
paperback *Passage to India* in my tweed jacket pocket were behind
us. I had arrived in Toronto for my post-secondary education at an
unfortunate moment in fashion. Everyone looked (and my mother
often pointed this out, in exactly these words) like a slob.

You couldn't tell the business students from the arts majors.
The law students all looked like they played in country bands. They
actually wore neckerchiefs. And so, amid this confusion, there
was no signal I could send out—no beret, no patched elbows—that
would let everyone know what I had in mind as a career.

I assumed that everybody in Professor Lindheim's class was as stymied by the fashion of the day as I was. I assumed that we were all there because, in various, perhaps not very precisely defined ways, we wanted to be writers.

This proved to be completely incorrect. Of course. Not everybody wanted to be a writer. In fact, nobody did. Law, mostly. A few into business. That's how wrong I was. It was the same thing with swimming pools.

I took it for granted that the old garden and the old view of the side of the escarpment and the old sounds of crickets and the old, distant shunting of boxcars, and the old feeling of slipping naked into the black water of a thick Hamilton midnight were foremost among my parents' assets.

I wondered aloud at the first of several meetings with my siblings and the real estate agent whether we shouldn't concede to potential home-buyers that they were probably going to demolish the house. This suggestion was met with no nods of agreement whatsoever from anybody.

I maintained that it was the setting and the presence of that old pool that justified our asking price. Speaking of which, I wasn't sure we were asking enough. I didn't think people understood just how (a search for a better word, but settling for) special the pool was.

"Oh, I think people understand," the real estate agent said pleasantly. "There are pictures on the website."

But of course that wasn't what I meant. And I told the real estate agent that if someone was interested in the property, genuinely interested but uncertain, I'd make them coffee early in the morning in my mother's kitchen, before dawn in fact, and I'd take them up through the dewy garden to the steps and the gate and the cabana where there is a surprisingly comfortable old chair and I'd show them the eastern sky lightening beyond the dark tumult of trees. And I'd show them how quiet the pool was at that time of day and what a good place it was to write. That could clinch a deal, I said. The real estate agent said she thought that it was a really great idea. She never mentioned it again.

Summer visits to Hamilton were more frequent than my trips in winter. My parents' house was draughty when it was cold, and it was always darker than I remembered. The room where our eighty-six, eighty-seven, eighty-eight-year-old mother sat and read the *Hamilton Spectator* every evening with a single glass of whisky used to be a room as bright as the palomino at the playroom window.

"What's in the news?" I'd ask her.

"Nothing good," she'd say.

This routine changed very little. We ate the same dinners. My mother always said: Let's order pizza. A medium Bianci from Capri. And it took me a while to realize that she didn't really like pizza. She thought I did, and she thought that ordering pizza would mean I wouldn't notice she didn't cook anymore. She told me the same stories. She always said I should sleep upstairs in one of the more comfortable rooms, and I always answered that I liked sleeping in my old bedroom in the basement. The same half-loaf of whole wheat bread was in the fridge. The same package of cheese slices. It was as if time was not passing. It was as if the black of charred elephant tusks was not lurking.

For a while we didn't tell my mother about Blake. It wasn't unusual for grandchildren to disappear for periods of time: for school, for travel, for work. But her grandchildren were very dear to her. She'd been a good mother. But she was a really good grandmother, and eventually she asked. And we told her in the most optimistic, no-big-deal, he's-still-editing, he's-still-producing, he's-still-composing terms we could muster. And I guess it worked. Because she forgot. Nothing bad was going to happen when I went to Hamilton. Nothing was ever going to change.

"Look at it this way," was what my friend had said to me when we sat on the lid of that culvert in the woods on the side of the Niagara Escarpment that summer and we were peaking. "Let's say you hear church bells."

As it happens, that's what we were doing. Hearing church bells. Coming up from the city below us. Probably St. Paul's Presbyterian on James Street, South, at Jackson.

"Peaking" was a misunderstood term. It implied a certain levelling out. In the case of the acid (windowpane) my friend had smuggled across the border in his Moroccan shoulder bag, there was not a whole lot of levelling out. Not for quite a long while. We were peaking, but only in the sense of peaking on a roller coaster.

Here is my friend's theory. I shall skip his preamble about Jung's interest in the *I Ching*.

We understand time the way we hear church bells. The highest point of volume catches our attention, but volume is just volume. It is, in fact, only one part of a rich harmony of fades and repeats and echoes. If you happened to be thinking (as we were), Whoa, this is really good acid, you could hear that intricate texture between the stroke of each hour quite clearly. Quite symphonically, actually.

My friend believed that there were dimensions of time that the businesslike components of the human brain successfully ignored. It would be (to use his precise terminology) far out for everything to happen at once. Because that's what everything was doing. Happening at once. If we were paying attention. Which we were. That night. Were we ever.

It's nice when things that I recognized as being important, or at least interesting, when I was young turn out to be important or at least interesting in (and there's no other way to describe the face in the painting, really) my later years. As an example: my friend thought there were coincidences so precise and yet so removed from utilitarian chronology it was impossible to think of them as fluke. They were visions of the future. They were entrances to the past. This kind of dime-store spiritualism was very popular, practically commonplace in those days, and so, of course, everybody makes great fun of it now. And yet, I have to say: the best evidence I ever encountered in support of my friend's view occurred almost fifty years after he expressed it. That was the night when Alison Gordon asked me to stay behind for a few minutes after band practice.

Much as Alison enjoyed the weekly presence of the band in her basement, there were limits. About two hours. Once a week. That was why it was unusual to be asked to stay behind. It had never happened to me before. And it never happened to me again.

And what she said to me was this: "Everybody will be all rah-rah with Blake. 'You're going to beat this,' they'll say. 'You'll be fine.' But somebody needs to tell him something else." Alison looked at me with an unusually intent and serious expression. She wanted me to hear what she had to say. "Otherwise he's all alone."

And this is where my friend's theory comes into play. This was one of those coincidences. Because it was later that night—later that same night, and you'll just have to take my word on that—after a rush to emergency, after a series of tests and scans and X-rays, after the results we'd been waiting for since long before midnight came back, after one of those endless stretches of white hospital time, that the doctors and nurses around Blake shifted into a new gear. They'd concluded he had a perforated bowel. They had to operate. Immediately. Things started to move very fast. "I'm frightened," Blake said to me. And thanks to my friend, Alison Gordon, I knew what to say.

"I am, too."

Every day, when I visited Blake, I went in the back door of the hospital, one block west of University Avenue. The narrow street is lined with high, modern medical institutions, one of which is Mount Sinai, the hospital where Caroline and Blake were born. The buildings loomed above me like cliffs.

I could never remember the name of that street. I'd look at the sign, and (as I discovered when friends asked for directions when they visited Blake) immediately forget it. Privately, I called it the valley. The valley of the shadow. The valley of the shadow of etcetera. And every day, as I approached the valley of the shadow of etcetera, I had to say (as in whisper the actual words to myself, out loud): Be brave. It was all I could manage, even though it was so much less than the bravery Blake required. That's why Glenfern was such a respite.

"I think I might go for a walk," I'd say to my mother on my visits to Hamilton. "Are you okay for a while?"

She reached for her scotch and water. She gave me a look over the newspaper. "I think I can probably manage."

In the early evenings of those October walks I liked the feel of the approach of November. And that's something else the painting captures: those reds, those browns, that orange. It was always there at that time of year in Hamilton: in the shadows of old trees; in the undersides of limestone cliffs. Hartman uses thick swirls of iron oxide to suggest this impending change of season. There was something bracing about it.

I zipped up my windbreaker against the crisp October evening and started down Glenfern Avenue at a solidly aerobic pace. And as I walked, I remembered things. Useless things mostly: the whereabouts of garden hoses, trash cans, clotheslines. I could picture back porches. I could remember old telephone numbers.

Breaks in hedges. Stones to be jumped. Hiding places. They were all still there.

I was fine with my visits to the Hamilton—the Hamilton you can see in the painting. During that period, I mean. In that general moment. Time didn't progress there, which was a relief. Except that I sometimes had work to do: magazine or newspaper assignments, deadlines to worry about. And when the weather got dark and cold there wasn't any place in my mother's house I liked to write very much. The desk in my old bedroom always made me feel like I was doing homework—to be read by Mr. Parsons with his impatient red pen in hand. So in the winter, when I visited Hamilton, my laptop and I would end up on Locke Street in Starbucks.

But summer was different. When I came to Hamilton for visits when it was warm (May and September: usually), or when it was hot (June, July, and August: always) I got into the habit of going to sleep when my mother did. Usually, by nine. But unlike my mother (who slept, she said, the sleep of the dead), I'd get up before sunrise. I'd make coffee. And then I'd find my way up from the back of the house, through the dew and darkness of the garden. Occasionally I'd startle one of the rabbits that had made its way down from the side of the escarpment.

At the top of the three steps at the end of the garden I juggled coffee and laptop. I found the key (hidden in the lantern my great-uncle Ed brought back from Japan in the early years of the twentieth century) and I opened the gate. I crossed the concrete patio.

The half-dozen mismatched chairs in the cabana were more stored than arranged by then. One of them, from an old patio set, was from my father's parents' time. It was vaguely art deco, and the slight rocking of its hooped steel legs made it surprisingly comfortable. Across from it, there was just enough width on the dusty windowsill for me to put my coffee. I put the Hamilton Tiger-Cats 1972 Grey Cup Champions cup between the water-testing kit and a sun-cracked deck-tennis quoit. I never had a better office.

18

The nurse seems always, in any room she is in, to be standing alone. But this could be the lighting.

The nurse speaks directly to camera. She says: Interior. Toronto house. Day.

She says: The weather has been horrendous.

The father's at home. This is downtown. He's looking out at the bleak view of a city in a snowstorm. He's on the phone and he's thinking, It's already the worst winter I can remember and it's only New Year's Day.

He offers to pick his wife up. She has called from the hospital to say their daughter has arrived for a shift and that he won't have to go in until later in the evening, and that she's going to walk home—along College and through the university campus. He points out the obvious to her: the weather is ridiculous. But she says she'd prefer to walk.

This is odd. The streets are plowed. They're both good winter drivers. They have snow tires. They pick one another up, drop one another off at the back of Princess Margaret all the time.

He sits down in front of the television in the third-floor bedroom but doesn't turn it on. The screen reflects the skylight's shifting grey. He squints at it. He wishes (as he often wishes these days) that the God of stained-glass windows was still with him.

He listens to the snow rattle against the glass doors of the third-floor bedroom. He falls asleep. He often does these days: sit down, fall asleep.

It's maybe twenty minutes later that he goes downstairs to make some tea. As he approaches the kitchen, he hears the back door open.

A mother steps into the light of the house. The noise of wind stops so abruptly she feels dizzy for a moment. And this is what you must understand. The nurse says. Directly to the reader.

This is a mother—a mother whose child is sick—who is coming in from that snowstorm. You don't need to know where she is from, or who she is, or the particular nature of her story. You could begin reading right here. She is a mother. That is all you need to know. She has no hat and no boots and her coat is brown cloth.

A blast of winter comes in with her. Her hair and shoulders are covered with snow. Her eyes are red and her cheeks are frozen and her sister who is visiting from Montreal asks, "How is he?" And she answers: "He's dying."

four

Before Pappy had his stroke nobody had ever heard him say anything much worse than damnation. So this came as a bit of a shock, especially to Granny. "Swearing like a trooper in his hospital bed," my mother said. "The nurses were terrified of him." He survived for a short while after. So we always picked Granny up for church.

Granny and Pappy had moved from Duke Street to a smaller place on Hess not long after the war. The new house was exactly two blocks from ours—if you were cutting through driveways and backyards to get there. If, however, you were driving to Granny's, as we were every single solitary Sunday morning as my mother sometimes pointed out, it was four blocks.

I could trace the route in the painting—at least, I could trace where I imagine it to be, and this is a point about that painting that I think should be made. It is not precisely articulated. Hartman's full brushstrokes of colour don't try to do the tiny stuff a camera can do just as well, if not better. And yet: put me in front of that painting and I could, if pressed, describe our Sunday morning route to Granny's house with what would seem obsessive detail. The painting (and this does seem a little miraculous to me, I have to admit) suggests the specifics that I happen to know are there.

That I remember those hedges and sidewalks and porches so clearly speaks to how established family routine was. I don't believe enough attention has been paid to how deeply the act of constant repetition influenced the mindset of the postwar middle class. We tended to do things over and over and over. It must be where we got the idea that nothing would end.

We had to pick Granny up on Sunday mornings at 10:30 on the dot. This, at any rate, was my mother's understanding of what had to happen ("Turn off that television. Get out of your pyjamas. Your father will help you with your tie.") Making breakfast and getting four children ready for church was a weekly routine that never seemed quite free of emergency. This had mostly to do with the grandfather clock ticking in my grandmother's vestibule. My mother was aware of the time from the moment she got up on Sunday morning. I didn't know what a nervous breakdown was, except it was what she said she was on the verge of by the time, finally, we were all in the car.

There are no details of that drive in the painting. But there is something in the thick greens and reds that allow for the possibility. The colours remind me: I know that route so well I could describe it as if I were looking at it from the side window of a blue Chevrolet station wagon.

Whether it was the stucco exterior or the low, horizontal profile, Granny's house had a vaguely film noir quality. In a movie it could be where Veronica Lake lived before a smooth-talking heel from Sacramento showed up. It wasn't modern, but it was somehow slightly modern. The house had a comfortable glamour—a characteristic that my grandmother did her best to subvert.

"Do you know the balloon lady?" is a good icebreaker if ever you find yourself speaking to someone with a keen interest in Royal Doulton figurines.

I am the oldest of four children, and so, on Sunday mornings, I was usually the one dispatched from the car. You can picture an astronaut setting out on a space walk.

Granny was waiting in a living-room chair adjacent to the front hallway and the grandfather clock. She was in her overcoat. She had her purse in her lap and her cane at her side. She wore hats that I remember being made mostly of small brown feathers. She smelled of toothpaste and lavender. She had a glass eye and a wooden leg.

Well, not wooden. But my father wasn't the kind of person who would say "artificial limb" unless he had to. Granny had somehow managed to hide her diabetes from Pappy until it was almost too late to save her life.

I was to ring once and step inside. So long as we arrived when we were supposed to the door would be unlocked. It couldn't have always been winter. But that's how I remember it.

"Good morning, young man," she always said. There was a slight tinkle of irony to this. Her expression conveyed that she was aware that this was a little bit funny because it was so exactly what an elderly woman of some grandeur would say upon the arrival of her grandson at her front door. And that's about as funny as Granny got. She had the kind of flat, trembling speaking voice that assured you she was a terrible singer.

Granny wasn't so much a mystery to me as she was someone I never thought much about because I couldn't imagine enough pertinent information about her to formulate a thought. I could never think of her getting dressed, for example. In my mind, Granny was clothed darkly and soberly at all hours of day and night. If I wondered what it was she did on Sunday mornings before I arrived at her front door, I didn't picture her dressing so much as getting fully rigged. Her dark pleated skirt and jacket and white blouse and black shoes and feathered hat and fox-head stole and cane and stately overcoat were like the proud display of a ship, all ensigns aloft.

She stood. She gathered herself. She made her way through the living room toward the front door. There was an ottoman and a what-not and a needle-pointed fireplace bench and a vestibule table and an umbrella stand to be navigated. I backed out the door I'd only partly entered.

She locked the front door behind her. She carefully secured the aluminum storm door. She opened her purse and unzipped its side-pocket. She deposited the door key. She zipped the side-pocket. And closed the purse. All this, in gloves.

Then came the icy stairs. They were made of exactly the hard, slippery brown tile that you would want to avoid at all costs if you had a wooden leg.

Granny clutched the wrought iron railing in her right hand. Her purse and cane occupied her left. This left me to flap around her, mostly uselessly, as assurance that should she slip at any point in her descent her well-mannered grandson would be ready to assist immediately.

On her front sidewalk Granny paused as one might pause at the bottom of a challenging ski hill. She caught her breath. She checked to make sure she'd put the door key back in the zipped side-pocket of her purse. And then we started across her front. Our car was waiting, idling warmly, in her driveway.

All this was fraught with peril—peril that I felt my father treated far too casually. If we'd had a radio in our car he would have been listening to it. He stared calmly over the steering wheel into the winter-blue sky while behind him a young boy and his one-legged grandmother were struggling across the steppe.

Church was a seven-block drive away. There was parking at the back of the church, which helped, but even so, getting Granny from the car to the narthex was a weekly adventure.

We managed, somehow. Every single, solitary Sunday until I went away to school, or Granny died, or something intervened to alter what had once seemed so unalterable, we managed to get Granny to church without mishap.

The light through those stained glass windows was impressive when the sun was out on those Sundays. That heavenly kingdom. Those flood waters and that open tomb. Once a week, Granny made her way under those raised roofbeams and through those shafts of glory to our customary pew at Melrose United Church. She leaned on my right arm. To port and starboard she bestowed an occasional nod to a familiar face.

2

A pool usually dominates a garden. In fact, in the fenced backyards of many North American middle-class neighbourhoods a swimming pool can pretty much *be* the garden. And this (so pool-owners are often reluctant to believe) can detract from the property's value. The problem is all the greater in Canadian residential markets where, for seven or eight months of the year, a pool in a garden is as attractive as a body wrapped for burial at sea. And that was exactly the point I tried to make to my siblings. I thought that one of the reasons the value of our pool was hard for real estate agents to calculate—one of the reasons our pool was special—was that it wasn't in the garden. I said this made all the difference in the world.

The pool was added to the garden. It was beyond the garden. It was an almost-vacant lot behind our back property line that had been owned by our next-door neighbour. And it was everything the garden wasn't. Flat, for one thing.

Our back garden was maintained by my father with more affection than design. And one of the garden's eccentricities was that it was on a slope. We were surrounded by gardens that had been levelled. But ours retained the angle of the escarpment's low-altitude beginnings—a fact my father's garden plans ignored.

Ne'er-do-well was a word my father liked. So was layabout. And both of these unsavoury types (ditto: unsavoury types) could be identified by their unkempt gardens. As a result, there was a sense of civic responsibility that prevailed in ours.

He liked the grass to be cut—not with the rolled, military precision on which a few of our neighbours insisted, but with some regularity. He liked the flowers to be approximately cared-for, the hedge to be trimmed now and then, the lawn to be watered when things got dry. He liked the invasive vegetation of the Niagara Escarpment to be kept more or less at bay. All this he did either by himself or with the help of his not-always-enthusiastic children. Weekends, usually.

There was no gardening tool that my father used that would have looked out of place in a Victorian potting shed. In fact several of them, inherited from his parents and probably grandparents, might have actually been Victorian. When I look at the horizontal brushstrokes of brown and orange that Hartman has used for the garden, I can't decide whether its slope is so precisely conveyed because of the artist's graphic skills or because I remember so well what it felt like to push an old, never-oiled, wooden-handled, revolving whir of rusted blades up it. I was sixteen by the time my father bought his first power mower.

I've been told that the first thing the new owners did was terrace the backyard, which makes sense. In my father's garden it was as if the bleeding heart and the Jacob's ladder and the peonies and the rose bush and the lawn had been put in place and then tilted. At the top of the slope a gloomy cedar hedge marked the end of our property—until the pool went in.

The walk to the pool—through the garden from the house— was uphill. At the steady pace that the lawn's incline dictated to everyone except children and Labrador retrievers, it took about a minute of slow, straight, uninterrupted walking to reach the old Japanese lantern on one side of the chain-link gate where the key to the padlock on the other side of the gate was kept.

It was not uncommon for my mother to be standing at the kitchen window with her coffee early on a summer morning and see one of her neighbours, in housecoat and slippers, walk uphill, through our garden, unlock the gate, and slip into the pool for a swim before work. "Your father has told the entire world where that key is," she'd say.

The ground cover (periwinkle) on the retaining wall (limestone) was the deep green Hartman uses. It seems like an older green. It's behind the swirls of sunnier, more contemporary foliage in the mid-ground of the painting.

Emergent from the ground cover in the southeast corner of the garden and acquired at a neighbourhood garage sale were five small, crumbling figures. Seven Dwarfs, approximately. Curiosities such as these were among the garden's quirks.

So was a ceramic bedpan my father planted with pansies every spring. And there was a strange, sextant-like piece of ophthalmological equipment that, when it appeared in a flower bed one summer in the nineties and I asked my mother what it was, she paused for a moment in her never-ending battle with the dandelions, patted her brow with the back of her gardening glove, sighed theatrically and said, "Ask your father."

3

We tell stories. Most families do.

It may have been that we put some special premium on telling them because I was in the business of writing stories. But I
don't think so, really. I think it was Janice's insistence that we all
eat dinner together. There was a period of time—ten or fifteen
years, I suppose—when friends or relatives who came to our
house were almost always jumbled together with the kids at the
table. Caroline and Blake grew up listening to people tell jokes,
describe situations, recount histories, argue points. So they did
the same. Stories—or the fragments of them that we passed back
and forth like familiar snapshots—were the background texture
to the bright, busy formlessness of that long-gone, apparently
endless present.

It wasn't because the story had to do with LSD that it sticks
in my mind—although an extremely powerful hallucinogen
does give a golf game a certain shimmer. Nor is it because those
eighteen holes represent one of the few occasions in my life I
spent more than a few minutes alone with my father. In fact, it's
not really the golf that stayed with me, to be honest, although
my game had its moments.

When I recall the round of father-son golf that was the unexpected grand finale to my night on the side of the escarpment
with my friend I don't immediately picture the Hamilton Golf and
Country Club course. Beautiful as it is. What first comes to mind is
the dinner table at our house in Toronto. It's me telling that story
that I see. I find that it's a good way to picture Blake.

The summer of my great LSD adventure was the summer that
I was working at the steel company. That was also the summer I
was taking golf lessons—a lifestyle choice my friend considered

cosmically hilarious. That's a quote. Cosmically hilarious. He'd been spending time in California.

I didn't object to golf lessons. I didn't object to golf. I was curious. I'd been doing some reading. This, like a lot of the best reading I've done in my life, was completely by accident. It was in whatever magazines people left behind in the cabana.

At first, I was curious about the byline, not the sport. If you were going to write about golf for *The New Yorker* you could hardly do better. If, to be more specific, you were going to write about golf in long, unhurried, occasionally digressive articles that appeared under the heading "The Sporting Scene" and, not only that, you were going to write about your subject in sentences and paragraphs and pages that were written with the same natural ease as someone playing a graceful, seemingly effortless eighteen holes, you couldn't have had a better name.

When my parents suggested golf lessons that summer, I pictured myself excelling quite easily at the game. How hard could it be? You stood in one place. You hit a ball. As well, I'd read Herbert Warren Wind, and therefore, quite apart from any natural athletic abilities I might bring to bear, I understood something of the poetry of the ancient sport, which was not generally true of junior members of the Hamilton Golf and Country Club.

My father didn't seem to really like playing golf all that much. I think he was happier vacuuming the pool. But sometimes he quite enjoyed it. Same with Rotary. Same with the committees at church. Sometimes golf was quite pleasant. Sometimes it wasn't. This was how things were.

But I will say this for golf. It played a big part in my dawning awareness that, as a general rule, it was a mistake to think anything will be easy.

"Let's see your swing then," the pro said. I'd told him that I thought I'd pick things up fairly quickly.

So that's how I came to be out at the Hamilton Golf and Country Club a couple of times a week. I only rarely played. I mostly just took lessons. And what I remember most clearly about those lessons is that there was nothing about a swing that was anything like I expected. Grip, position, rhythm—all came as news. Compared to the general mechanics of a slapshot in ball hockey, which was the model on which my initial confidence was based, the golf stroke proved to be complicated.

So, that's how it happened that I was taking golf lessons the same summer that my friend was doing what we both took to be the very opposite of taking golf lessons. I was finding the key to the swing elusive. He was finding the open road. I was trying to open my hips squarely. He was making his serendipitous, psychedelic way back and forth across America. We enjoyed our unlikely juxtaposition.

The pro was trim and ramrod straight. His tanned, leathery skin made his age impossible to guess. He brought a certain military authority to a tee. His checked pants were much the same blue as my madras Bermuda shorts. My knee socks (formerly my father's) were the colour of putty. It took me three attempts to make contact with the ball.

4

When I was taught how to swing a driver by the golf club's leathery pro I was taught the modern stroke. Naturally. With modest local variation, everybody is taught the modern stroke—and what's interesting about the modern stroke (apart from the gracefully calibrated, disciplined efficiency of its movement) is that it was more or less invented by J. Douglas Edgar.

Edgar had a gamey hip. It was what gave his pace of walking around a golf course its happy jaunt. And in order to compensate for his inability to swivel around on a tee like a hula dancer, he developed the stillness of shoulders and hips through which the acceleration of his club head would pass. This proved to be an astonishing fulcrum of energy. He called it the gateway, and foremost among the gateway's remarkable qualities is this: it is simultaneously the easiest and the hardest thing in the world to do. It's easy because when you do it right it feels perfectly natural. Hard because doing it right is what most players hardly ever do.

I recently read that in the 1950s the British Army conducted experiments with LSD, and what the British Army discovered was that the drug's tactical applications were limited. The volunteers did nothing but laugh. Uncontrollably. And much the same thing happened to my friend when I told him about my golf lessons. I think it was my mentioning Bermuda shorts and beige knee socks that set him off. We were sitting on top of a water culvert, in the woods, on the side of the Niagara Escarpment at the time. Cosmically hilarious. I thought he was going to hurt himself.

So that must have been the summer I read *The Doors of Perception* and *Be Here Now* and *The Teachings of Don Juan* and *The Psychedelic Experience*. These were my friend's recommendations. He wrote quotes from each of them on the backs of postcards.

He was on the road—hitchhiking through the United States. This was part homage to our favourite writer, Jack Kerouac, and part investigation into certain high-performance psychedelics unavailable in Canada. It was not clear to me how he did this: it required a particular talent to arrive unannounced and unknown in an American city, bypass all the shitty mescaline, speed-laced blotter and crappy MDA, and end up crashing with far-out people who were into yoga, and macrobiotic food, and some amazingly pure and powerful LSD.

The message on the back of the first postcard, in my friend's terrible handwriting: *"Time is an illusion"—Albert Einstein*. The photograph on the front a city skyline: Greetings from St. Louis.

Even if we didn't plot exactly when we would intersect that summer, we were somehow confident that we would—"somehow" being a bigger part of people's thinking in those days. A long-distance call was as rare as a telegram.

As that summer passed—as I saved my steel company money for university; as I plowed through Hemingway; as I (in madras shorts and putty-coloured knee socks) got a feel for my three-wood and my seven iron—my friend and I shared a sense that things would work out without being too specific about what working out might mean.

"Be here, now!"—Baba Ram Dass. Souvenir of Joplin, Missouri.

"However expressive, symbols can never be the things they stand for"—Aldous Huxley. A Souvenir of Travelodge, Barstow, California.

My friend's travels would culminate, somehow, in his arrival. Here, I figured. In Hamilton. Now.

My father said things like: "Can you explain to me how your friend dropped out of high school and got into college?" Or: "What is it that your friend does for money?" Or (when I got back from a double shift at the steel company that summer afternoon): "Your friend has arrived from somewhere. He's down in your room. He said he wanted to crash."

"Crash" is pronounced as if another language.

"He hitchhiked. Evidently."

And if it wasn't that summer—that full, thick summer; that summer when the universe seemed to align itself so naturally with being young—let's say it was. There were a few of them that were very much the same. And anyway, Hartman's perspective is not perfectly realistic, either. He's looking for some essence of city that is not beholden to its grid of streets. You can read whatever you want to read into Hartman's representation of Hamilton. It's like the *I Ching* that way. The absence of order is the order. That's what looking at a painting is. It's quite a lot like acid, to be perfectly honest.

5

It was a blazing day, my mother said. The children could perish in the heat.

There were patches of sunshine back there in the garden of my parents' house—a spray of sap-green across darker foliage. This seemed to be how gardens were lit when I was a child. The afternoon sunshine made its fractured way through the trees. And the light (filtered; dappled) was behind the proud young mother in a pretty summer dress with the Kodak camera.

The garden's shade was something on which my mother often commented. But this was like commenting (as she also often did) on Hamilton's infernal summer heat. There wasn't much to be done about it—not until sometime in the 1980s, when her complaints coalesced into a campaign to open the back to more sunlight.

"Your mater finds that row of pine trees depressing," my father said, as if reporting on a force that he was unable to explain but that would, so he could see, prevail.

The garden was made much brighter. There was still a big maple, and the quince tree, and some ash. Our neighbours had big, old trees. The whole side of the escarpment was nothing but. So there were still lots of trees—it's just that the garden caught a bigger, longer, square of sunshine than it used to, a change that has made it always feel to me as if the garden our children knew when we came for visits in the summer was quite a different place from the back garden I knew when I was growing up.

All that blazing afternoon we'd been swimming—although "swimming" was an activity of which actual swimming was only a part. It also included sitting with my parents, watching the kids, getting the lemonade from the fridge in the house, lying in the sun for a while, reading for a bit, and maybe falling asleep for a few minutes in the chaise between the black-current bushes. And now, while Caroline assists her grandmother in her war on the dandelions, and Janice reads, Blake and I are playing catch in exactly the spot where my father once played catch with me. Young fathers are very susceptible to sentimentality of this sort.

I could show you in the painting where this happened and I could describe the exact texture of that afternoon. I could trace the arc of that ball back and forth. *Wa-un. Two-oo. Three-ee.* The numbers are stretched out to accommodate the slow, underhanded tosses. The game we are playing is how high we can count before missing one. I played the same game with Caroline although she's too big for that now.

I could explain how the angle of the sun gave everything exactly the colour of summer. I don't think there's a detail I can't bring to mind, including the smell of my son's hair when I picked him up and gave him a hug. We'd got almost to twenty.

There was an entire garden between the back of the house and the gate to the pool—a garden big enough to accommodate grandmothers yanking up weeds, and granddaughters helping. Big enough to include fathers and sons playing catch and grandfathers watering the tomatoes. Big enough for dogs and Frisbees and were you writing the property up for a real estate advertisement you could call it generous. This was no abbreviated garden. And that, so I argued (to no avail), made all the difference. The single most important characteristic of the pool was that it was removed from things. Were you to measure from where the garage used to be, then add the full distance of a lawn sprinkler's arc, and then calculate the space of open, golden light required by a parent and a child to play a decent game of catch—the total of all that would be how far the pool was from our house. The blue was only visible from the second floor. If there had been a baby born up there nobody would have heard a thing.

6

John Hartman said he wanted to hike along the wooded trail near the top of the steep wooded slope behind my parents' house. He wanted to find a vantage point for a portrait of Hamilton, Ontario, Canada. He wanted to take some photographs for reference. Sometimes he uses a drone to get the aerial views he likes. He wanted to scout possible launch sites.

I don't remember any discussion of my being in the picture while we were on our walk. But that doesn't mean the conversation didn't take place. I was distracted by what was going on with Blake. And I was distracted by my parents' house. It wasn't the easiest sale.

The challenge was this: we were selling a piece of real estate with a personality that, much like its wiring, was planted firmly in the centre of the twentieth century. It was a property so replete with memento and so in need of renovation that any cosmetic improvement only made matters worse.

It was my idea that instead of trying to disguise my parents' interiors we should curate them. Instead of gussying them up with alien furniture and throw pillows, we should display them as what they almost were anyway: artifacts. We'd be archivists. It seemed more dignified.

I thought we should decorate each room as per a particular period of our family's history.

Here, I'd say.

This was my youngest brother's bedroom during his Hot Wheels phase; this is what the den looked like when my father and my sister and my other brother watched *M*A*S*H* after dinner; this was my bedroom in the basement (Humphrey Bogart and W. C. Fields posters on the fake-wood panel walls; *Beggars Banquet* on the Seabreeze turntable, *Seventeen* magazine under my bed); this is my mother's telephone table in the kitchen, piled with calendars and invitations and Junior League directories and art gallery annual reports and the notes she scribbled on a spare prescription pad of my father's endless supply (Dr. E. Blakely Macfarlane, Suite 610, Medical Arts Building, 527-1282). There was a telephone that was a colour my mother described as beigey-pink. There was a jar full of ballpoint pens, few of which worked. There was *The I Hate to Cook Book*. There was *Phyllis Diller's Housekeeping Hints*. There was a framed *Peanuts* cartoon: Snoopy on the meaning of life. The house was at its peak in the 1970s. In the kitchen: orange and brown, predominantly.

My idea was met not so much by the real estate agent's disapproval as her polite bemusement. Part of her job, of course, is to be pleasant. She smiled as she probably often smiled at clients.

She suggested a more *commercially attuned* approach. She had a gift for speaking in italics.

The place needed work. Here and there. That was clear. But that's always true of properties that are *unique*.

The windows were draughty. The laundry room was a dungeon. But these are the upgrades you have to expect to make in a building with *history*.

This was the kind of home that you almost never see on the market anymore. It was the real estate agent's idea that it should be advertised as "The Doctor's House."

7

He was operating. He was doing rounds. He was at the office. He was on call.

In the years when my father's occupation was spoken of in the present tense, these general explanations of his whereabouts were how our family kept track of his comings and goings. He was a slightly distant figure, not because he was cold or indifferent, but because he actually was distant to us a lot of the time. His car backed down the driveway early in the morning. It returned (with the same little burst of gravel at the sidewalk) sometimes for a half-hour lunch, sometimes not until the end of a busy day.

When my father was at work he was at work. It was mostly a routine we never witnessed. We only caught glimpses.

His black bag in the front hallway. His stethoscope when we asked if he'd let us hear our own heartbeats. He had a human skull in the cupboard above his dressing-room closet—a souvenir that somehow his father had acquired at medical school—and what's odd about that, so it seems to me now, is that none of us found this odd at all. An actual human skull was just there, beside the Johnson & Johnson tin of first-aid supplies. A skull being one of those things doctors had: like mercurochrome, like gauze, like suture.

It was his unruffled bedside manner as much as his professional training that made him the administrator of our family first aid. He brought a certain calm to the crises of scraped knees and chickenpox. There is still a crease above my right eye where, without much fuss (my mother aghast), he stitched me up after a fall from a tricycle. The scar is only visible if I point it out. You can just see it in the painting, although it could be a crease in my forehead with no particular history.

It's a memento of my father that I have: the smell of his shaving soap as he bent closely over my face. I remember he pulled the suture tight with a surprising lack of daintiness, much the way he laced my ice skates. Much the way, as things turned out, that I laced Caroline's and Blake's.

When I was young—young enough to be holding my father's hand as he led me down the long, polished hallways of the Hamilton General Hospital—I was proud when people called him Doctor. And people often did. "Yes, Doctor." "No, Doctor." "Good morning, Doctor."

I liked telling kids (at school, at Cubs, at church, at the Y) what my father did for a living. And as I recall (so I told Blake when he asked about this point), I don't think what my father earned had anything to do with my pride. For one thing, I had no idea what my father earned. I just thought a doctor was a very good thing for a father to be.

One of the characteristics of the class in which I grew up (somewhere between the middle and the upper sections of the middle class) was that the relative affluence of the postwar years co-existed with a frugality inherited from both the Depression and the War.

As a result, about as precise as I could be about our economic station was that we were not poor. Of course this was preposterous—as Blake's stare made clear when I told him this in the hospital one bright, white day. Compared not only to most of the rest of the world, but, in fact, compared to almost every human who had ever lived, we were wildly, unimaginably wealthy.

My father's retirement party was held in the back garden. I could describe that garden to you while standing in front of the painting and pointing to the umber and muted oxides of the lawn.

Later in the evening, guests moved into the living room. They ate (as was always the case in the living room) on their laps. Beef stroganoff. Madame Benoît's recipe. Clipped years before from the (now defunct) *Canadian* magazine.

And then, after we cleaned up and put the party glasses away, I began to forget about my father.

I had not imagined that his retirement would change anything—and in certain ways it didn't really change very much. He dressed a little more casually than he used to. Cardigans more often than suit jackets. But he still went to Rotary. He still delivered fruitcake to the halt and to the lame at Christmas. He retained the kindly formality of an attending physician.

This was a slow and gradual shift that played out over many, many family birthdays and Christmases. I can't now imagine how there were so many.

I suppose it took a few years, but at some point I stopped calling him Dad. Without giving the transition any thought, I started calling him Grandad—largely so our kids and our nieces and nephews would know to whom I was referring. He became for me what he was for our children: beloved, unhurried, funny. Grandad. I gradually stopped thinking of him as the busy doctor who held my hand in those enormous corridors.

The wings of Hamilton General Hospital, as seen in the painting, are brackets of cold grey about halfway between the top of my head and the flat cobalt of Hamilton Harbour. That's how the hospital is now, of course—far different from the buttery incandescence that I remember when my father took me with him on his rounds. There were gold letters stencilled on frosted glass. There were green blotters on desks. There were black, rotary telephones.

But everything is different now. Everything is brighter, for one thing.

8

The reason I was allowed to fluff the cabana was that it probably wouldn't make a difference anyway.

"Don't say 'fluff,'" Blake said. "It's a horrible word."

So, I said, okay. "How about 'staging'?"

The reason I could stage the cabana was that it would have no bearing, one way or the other, on the sale of the house.

It was dusk when I was finished. I sat at the far end of the pool and looked back to the cabana's glow in the dark glen of water and trees and sky. The brown light, surrounded by the stillness of black ironweed with the violet sky beyond, was like a Magritte painting— or (to be perfectly honest about my credentials as an art critic) like the Jackson Browne album cover that borrows from a Magritte painting. I listened to that album a lot one summer. I now wonder how it was that my parents never smelled anything. Lebanese blonde, usually. Occasionally, when I was lucky, black Moroccan.

What I retained in the cabana (the wicker coffee table, the seahorse-shaped ashtray) and what I added to the cabana (a cocktail shaker and two light-plaid, beach-house-style swivel chairs that I found in the rec room) had to conform to the general aesthetic of what that space was like when it was new. Or what I remembered it was like. Or maybe just what I thought I remembered it was like the summer I listened to that Jackson Browne album so much, which was, I'm pretty sure, the same summer a girl I'd met in Professor Lindheim's class came over from Toronto on the bus for weekend visits.

Naturally, my mother told me to put out the guest towels. In the guest bedroom. This left the pool.

The weightlessness of the shallow end and the fact that the underwater lights hadn't worked for years did nothing to diminish my fondness for that big old pool. Night swims were always nice. Sometimes extremely nice. Hartman was absolutely right to make the pool's aquamarine pizzazz central to my portrait. I can't deny it.

"That girl has legs for days," my mother remarked. And it was true. That girl did. And when she first stepped out of the change room that particular Hamilton summer, she stopped there, frozen with shyness, as if she had become suddenly aware of how beautiful she was.

I was standing in the shallow end at the time, and I was the witness to a change-room exit that, in its graceful balance of towel and bikini, could have been a movie poster. Had I been called upon to explain to the real estate agent what I wanted to do when I staged the cabana, I might have attempted to describe what that young woman looked like coming out of the change room that day, but fortunately I never had to. Nobody really cared what I did up at the pool.

The ritual of selling a piece of long-held real estate had the same futility grief can have. So I noticed. I'd never previously made the connection, but my father had died a few years before, my mother more recently. Grief and grieving, words I had managed to avoid most of my life, were subjects of books well-meaning neighbours now dropped off for us to read, and from my vantage point (at the pool's far end; after the day I spent staging the cabana) I could see that the emptying of my parents' old house was part of the same never-satisfactory process of saying goodbye.

It was a ritual, and as in funerals, the ritual had a great, big, hard-to-wrap-your-head-around absence at its core. My siblings and I divided up those things that belonged to my parents that we wanted to keep (gout stool, what-not, balloon lady), but the house and the garden and the pool and the cabana might as well have been a box of ashes by then. It was the same thing when my father was in the hospital.

"There's nothing semi-private about it," my mother said. "It's like Grand Central in there."

When my father spoke from the bed of his semi-private room in Hamilton General Hospital his collegial manner with his nurses and doctors reminded me what he'd been like when I used to walk down those hallways, my hand in his. I'd almost forgotten. "Good morning, Doctor." "How are you, Doctor?" He seemed to know everything about that hospital.

But when he was in that same hospital as an old man, and not as a medical practitioner, as a patient and not as a physician, and his eldest son came to visit, I couldn't tell the nurses from the doctors from the cleaners from the food-service workers. But he knew who everyone was and what their particular relationship was to the condition—failing—in which he found himself.

My father was never good with names socially. I've inherited this weakness. But I noticed that in the hospital he knew the name of every nurse. And he used their names every time he asked for something, or thanked them for something, or answered their questions, or said good morning.

Blake had the same capacity. It seemed to come naturally to him, out of the blue. Because it's not as if he'd had any practice.

I was surprised by this talent, at first—but only because I never seem to learn the names of people I don't know well and because fathers very often think sons are more like them than they are.

Blake had a familiar, friendly manner with nurses, and for some reason (possibly because I saw it happen so many times over the four and a half years of his illness) it's one of the best ways I know to bring Blake's laughter to mind: to picture how his face looked when he shared some little joke with a nurse who was changing an IV unit or checking his vitals.

My heart could burst. I used these exact words. I used them to myself, but I used them, consciously, as I sat in that room, in that light, and watched how he conducted himself with the people who were doing what they could to help him. He was laughing. Despite everything, he was laughing in a friendly, easy way. The nurse liked him. You could tell. And as I sat there I actually said to myself: I am so proud of you my heart could burst.

My father listened to what the nurses and doctors and residents and interns who gathered around his bed had to say, and he agreed or disagreed with their assessments in what sounded more like a discussion among professionals than the delivery of a not-very-promising prognosis to an elderly patient. And it didn't surprise him when things got worse. That's what he would have predicted had anyone asked.

It's like watching a storm gather. At first it's on the horizon, purple and dark, but the prevailing wind is blowing the other way, as it generally does, so you think the bad weather will pass you by. But it doesn't. The storm has its own direction. It has its own internal momentum. It doesn't matter what the prevailing wind is doing. Fifteen minutes later the thunder is all around you.

My father had a series of small strokes. It became difficult for him to speak. He had no interest in food. Once, when I asked him the name of a Hamilton church I drove past every day on my way to visit him at Hamilton General, he was surprised to find he couldn't remember.

"Just across Bay Street from Central Public School," I said, hoping to jog his memory. "Red brick."

I'm not sure I ever in my life saw him look so sad. And when it fell to me to tell him of some last-ditch effort his medical team was proposing, he moved his head back and forth on the pillow as firmly as he could. He was a doctor after all. "No further treatment," he said. And that was that.

9

"I have realized that the past and future are real illusions, that they exist in the present, which is what there is and all there is"—Alan Watts. Greetings from San Bernardino, California. So that would have been the summer my friend showed up in Hamilton.

My friend arrived in time for my birthday, not that he had any idea when my birthday was, so far as I know. Because this would have been when I picture him there, up at the pool, sitting with my parents in the cabana eating birthday cake.

My father had gone grey and mostly bald when he was still a young man. This was probably a useful disguise, at first. His formality with senior colleagues must have reinforced the impression that he was older than he was. It wasn't until his fifties that the way he looked started to coincide with his age.

In dress, in manners, and in his general comportment my father was stubbornly, at times almost radically, conventional.

Suit, white shirt, tie, decent shoes. This was what he wore to work every day. His recreational attire was similarly unsurprising. In acknowledgement of the age of Aquarius, his sideburns were gradually lengthening. He looked exactly like you'd think an ophthalmologist in Hamilton, Ontario, in the 1960s would look.

In the cabana that evening he was in a tapered, pale blue polyester sports shirt. My mother: her hair golden, a summer dress.

They had served the hamburgers my father had just grilled on the hibachi. My father's hamburgers tended to be extremely well-done. But they were tasty enough when slathered with lots of ketchup. My friend ("Go ahead," my mother said, "you must be starving") had three.

Earlier that afternoon my mother pointed out, several times, that it was "a hundred and ten in the shade." If the temperature had dropped by dinner it hadn't dropped much. It was a hot, sticky Hamilton summer evening and yet my friend was wearing a full-length denim coat. But that was an interesting thing about my friend. It didn't seem to matter. The coat, the shoulder-length hair, the beads—were things my friend had the ability to ignore. He seemed to be entirely untroubled by how unusual he looked in the context of bamboo furniture, tapered golf shirt, sundress, and an ashtray shaped like a seahorse—an ashtray shaped like a seahorse that he was slowly filling with butted Marlboros. He could not have been more congenial.

He was very good at talking with parents—and university registrars and border guards. His apparently sincere interest in what adults had to say was disarming. Only the occasional eyebrow raised briefly in my direction indicated that he was engaged in some fairly tricky high-wire stuff, conversationally speaking. He'd been on very good LSD for pretty much his entire journey from the Pacific coast.

"And you hitchhiked?" my mother asked as pleasantly as her alarm at the idea would allow.

"From San Francisco," my friend assured her just as pleasantly. "Four rides."

After we'd helped with the dishes, and while my parents were watching television in the den, we set off. "Don't be too late," my mother called out. We went a little ways along Beckett Drive and then left the road, climbing up into the long shadows of the woods.

It wasn't so much like stepping out of the map of time as flying over it: as if Hamilton, beautiful as it appeared on that glittering, psychedelic adventure, on that long-ago summer night, wasn't a city at all. It was a network of intersections—a surveyor's grid of seconds and minutes and eons over which I was gliding. We could see beyond the necklace of lights over the Skyway Bridge and beyond the flares at the steel mills. We could see beyond the shimmering lake toward the glow of Toronto on the far horizon. Obviously past and future were illusions. Obviously there was only the present.

It was windowpane. Early windowpane to be precise. A year later you couldn't find acid like that anymore.

10

When my father was a boy, a trip from Hamilton to Toronto by motor car was more of a journey than it was for us. These outings (undertaken by his parents with their four children) were more family obligation than recreation. There were aunts and uncles to be visited in Toronto. My father, as per the evidence of several photographs, often wore a sailor suit.

The journey to Toronto when my father was a child was often bumpy and dusty. It was always long. But it was not without its pleasures. The trip would involve a stop somewhere along the Dundas Highway or Lake Shore Road for tea or ice cream. Sometimes they stopped for luncheon. There were cut-glass bowls of carrot sticks and goblets of ice water. The waitresses wore pale-blue uniforms and white aprons. There were long spoons for sundaes. This was how things used to be.

A stop on the way to or from Toronto was not absolutely required. But a break was a welcome, civilized part of the ritual. And that, on its own, is a distinction between my generation and my father's. He inhabited a time when there was a texture between places in southwestern Ontario that would mostly disappear by the time his children made the journey. On our way from Hamilton to Toronto we never stopped anywhere.

"That restaurant?" I asked him, not long before he died.

From as early in my life as I can actually remember I'd worried about my parents' deaths. There was one summer (long before the pool) when we went to a lodge on Lake of Bays for a week in a rented cabin, and there was something about the shadows of the rafters and the smell of wood that filled me with dread every night of our holiday. "Oh, don't be so silly," my mother would say, "that won't happen for a long, long time." And now that a long, long time has happened, I realize how much I'll miss my father's odd, un-researchable memories of Hamilton. Who else would tell me that Mrs. Hendrie's chauffeur kept a footstool in the car so that he could more gracefully assist in her exit from the back seat when she attended a ladies' tea at the art gallery? Who else would be shocked that I didn't know the way to Webster's Falls or the Waterdown market?

My father knew the geography that you can see in the Hartman painting. He knew it very well.

"The restaurant your family used to stop at coming back from Toronto," I asked. "What was it called? The one near Aldershot. Or Burlington. Or somewhere . . ."

My father always professed to be shocked at my ignorance of the very many extremely interesting and well-known places that were once part of the trip between Hamilton and Toronto. "Are you some kind of knucklehead?"

Getting to know my father was a long process. Sixty years, in my case—but the fact that he was a slow reveal was not because he was unkind.

My father wasn't withholding. He wasn't coldly silent. It's just that he was untroubled by the gaps that existed between his speaking one sentence and then speaking the next. Getting to know my father took a while. That's all. And one of the things about him that became more clear to me as I grew older was that he recalled details of his childhood with an enthusiasm that seemed unrelated to his natural disinclination to speak.

"Oh, you mean the Estaminet," he answered, as if producing the missing piece of a jigsaw.

The Estaminet restaurant was where his family used to stop on their semi-regular Toronto excursions. I could describe it in some detail, which is odd since I was never in it. But it's a memory I feel I have because it was such a clear memory of my father's. It was the kind of dining room (cream of celery soup, chicken pot pie) that doesn't exist anymore, with lemonade swirling in its mixer, with pewter parfait cups piled with whipped cream and a maraschino cherry, and with the dusty road beyond the gravel parking lot. Before the highway, when things moved more slowly, this was the way to Toronto. Oh, and the light was different somehow.

The sketched forms of houses that are to the right of my head in Hartman's painting have a quality of invisibility. It's as if only the uprights and crossbeams are present. The houses look as if a viewer could peer down into the attics and back stairs and hallways. This was, in fact, a convention of Japanese painting in the fifteenth century—no more unrealistic, I suppose, than the way a movie is cut. Establishing shot: exterior. Then, interior.

You could think of these sketches as a kind of shorthand for a neighbourhood, I suppose—although it happens to be shorthand I read well. I know every chenille bedspread, every laundry hamper, every wrinkle in the wall-to-wall. I know where every telephone is mounted in every kitchen. I know every driveway and backyard shed. I know every hedge and clothesline. The detail is there. In the painting's imaginative space. I can assure you of that.

So let me just put it this way. That windowpane was extremely pure and extremely strong. By way of summary: the night unfurled and kept unfurling. By the time the sun was coming up, I realized I had to impose some order on what was happening. If we got back to the house too late my parents would be awake, and my mother would probably want to know what we'd been doing. For the entire night. In the woods.

Eventually I got my friend down from the side of the escarpment. He was telling me something important about Carl Jung and didn't want to be interrupted. But finally I got him to shut up. Finally, I got him stowed away in an empty bedroom on the second floor of my parents' house. I was still as high (entirely accurate description) as a kite.

It must have been shortly before six o'clock. And I decided that the best thing for me to do would be to go down to my bedroom in the basement. Close the door. Turn off the light. Get into bed. I didn't have to go back in to the steel company until eleven the following morning. I was hoping that by then I'd be fine.

Sleep was out of the question. But pretending to sleep seemed the best way to avoid interaction with other humans for the time being. I thought it best to lie low until the breakfast routines of my parents and my brothers and sister were out of the way on the floor above me.

Later in the morning, I might come upstairs to the empty kitchen and see about having a glass of orange juice. Orange juice was supposed to help. Maybe I'd go for a swim, although one had to be careful about pools. Brian Jones and all.

But that's not what happened.

What happened was the last thing I was expecting to happen: what happened was that, not long after I'd got into bed, I heard my father come down the stairs from the second floor to the bathroom on the ground floor that he used in the mornings. This wasn't unusual. This is what he did every morning. What was unusual was what he did next.

I was familiar with the weight and cadence of my father's steps. Living in the basement (and being a teenager and doing things I didn't want anyone to find me doing) made me acutely aware of the doors, voices, clocks, flushed toilets, vacuum cleaners, telephones, radio, and footsteps of the house's daily and (usually) predictable soundscape. I kept track of arrivals and departures by the slight, inadvertent jangle the bell at the side door made whenever the door was opened or closed, or the clatter of my mother's shoes in the hardwood hallway as she hurried to a ringing telephone. I knew the click on the control of the washing machine when my mother put in a load of laundry, and I could recognize the slow sliding of a spoon around an aluminum pot of milk that meant my father was making one of the few things he knew how to make in the kitchen: yogurt, oddly. The sound of my mother grabbing the car keys from the kitchen drawer was a distinctively brief combination of rattled wood and jangled metal before the drawer was banged shut and the keys were silenced, with an equally distinctive plop, by the snap of her purse. I could identify everyone in the family by the sound of their footwear and the speed with which they moved on the floors above me.

So when my father started down the basement stairs I knew what was happening. I just couldn't explain it.

For my father to visit my bedroom was unusual. I will go so far as to say: highly unusual. My father rarely ventured near, and never in the early morning.

But now something even more improbable was happening. He was opening my door.

My mind wasn't racing. More accurately, my brain was ransacking its own interior—dumping out the drawers of recent memory and throwing open the closets of possibility, trying to find some explanation for why my father was doing what he was doing. And while all this was going on I lay still, under the covers, my eyes tightly shut. I exaggerated the slow rhythmic breathing of sound sleep as best I could.

As you might imagine, the overhead light was extremely bright. Atomic bomb bright. Exploding sun bright. And it felt to me as if the moment's inexplicability was the fuel for this blinding event. What crack in the universe had I fallen through that allowed me to see something (my father, in my bedroom) for which I had no explanation?

I was still a few hours away from even beginning to come down. I was still unable to see my hand reaching for my alarm clock (as if the correct time of day would help me understand what was going on) without seeing after-traces of my hand's movement in the brilliant, shimmering air.

Surely he would see my surprise. Surely he would realize he'd made some mistake. What was he thinking barging into my room in what was practically the middle of the night? Surely he'd say sorry, flick off the light, back out, and everything would go back to the way it was supposed to be. But: no.

He was saying I'd better get up and at it. He was saying: Come on, shake a leg.

My father wanted to know: Had I forgotten?

We were playing golf. It was my mother's idea, really. But there you go.

12

Blake asked me about the horror movies I'd watched. I remember having this conversation with him on the College street-car. Westbound. We'd just seen a horror movie, as it happened. *It.* At the Carlton. It was the last movie I went to with Blake. And I was telling him that one of the things I liked about the neighbourhood in Hamilton in which I grew up was that it was so easy to imagine horror movies happening in it. It was like living on a studio lot. There's the gothic turrets of the haunted house. There's the suburban bungalow where the zombies break through the picture window. There's the place behind the Bates Motel.

Did I want to go to a movie? Blake had asked earlier that day. And if I may, I'll offer a word of advice. If your child asks you to go to a movie, go. No matter what you are doing. Go.

We'd often gone to movies together over the years, a pretty typical list, I suppose, when he and Caroline were younger. We hadn't gone since he got sick. But he looked pretty good. He was feeling pretty well. In Hamilton, when I was a kid, we called it going to the show.

I grew up in a neighbourhood that ended where the steep, tangled slope of the Niagara Escarpment began. The woods were a little wild. There were ravens. Well, crows, actually. But we liked to think of them as ravens. There was Jacob's Ladder, and there were trails that snaked through snarls of underbrush. There were dry, rocky creek beds. There was poison ivy and there were creeping vines. There were shattered pieces of the foundations of a long-abandoned railway incline that looked like the remnants of moats and drawbridges. There were caves. And the remains of mysterious campfires. There were storm sewers that, so long as there were no storms, could be explored. And, at the top of the limestone outcroppings and trickling waterfalls, there was exactly what you'd expect to find looming over a quiet, ordinary middle-class neighbourhood in a late-night horror movie: an insane asylum. That's what we called it.

The Ontario Hospital commanded a promontory of the mountain brow. This was pretty much directly above my parents' house. It had been built in 1875—an institution originally intended for the rehabilitation of alcoholics but soon dedicated to the treatment and incarceration of "demented minds and lunatics."

We always wondered what went on behind those brick walls, and in the fall of 1968, when the original Victorian structure was being torn down to be replaced with more modern psychiatric facilities, one of my brothers and I crossed Beckett Drive one Sunday afternoon and climbed up the trails through the woods to the hospital. There. I can show you the path. It's in the upper right of the Hartman painting.

We hurried across the asylum's lawn. We made our way over a rubble of brick into the derelict building. And we were surprised to discover that many of the cells really were padded. They really did have restraints in the walls. "I thought we were making that stuff up," my brother said.

When I was young, the asylum cast a shadow of rumour over the woods that tumbled down to the streets of our neighbourhood from the edge of the hospital's lawn: rumours of escaped inmates and lost psychopaths. It was believed that there was a siren that would go off when a patient went missing—a belief undiminished by the fact that we never once heard it.

The side of the escarpment was where children playing in the woods found the torso of Evelyn Dick's estranged husband. Actually, this was in the woods a few miles to the west of our stretch of the mountain, but we overlooked these details of geography. His arms, his legs, and his head had been incinerated in the furnace of Evelyn's east-end Hamilton home. At her sensational trial (two sensational trials, actually; she was sensationally acquitted on appeal after being sensationally sentenced to hang in 1946) it was contended that she had tried to bury what remained of John Dick's body on the side of the escarpment after she'd chopped off his arms, his legs, his head.

How could you?

Mrs. Dick.

I got the joke. Eventually. It was a while later, that same fall. In Current Events, and somebody held up the picture of the wincing Lee Harvey Oswald, and Gary or Kingsley or Herbert or somebody whispered, "How could he miss his dick?"

"What's so funny over there?" said Mr. Parsons.

The transition from night to daytime vision is called the

Purkinje shift, and the effect can be something like the strange lighting of old horror movies. In our living room, with no lights on, it makes the background of Hartman's painting appear to be getting darker for a moment, even while ambient light from the windows grows very, very slowly brighter with dawn. And if you are my age you can think: Fuck, I'm having a stroke. Because it always feels to me as if this contradiction has more to do with my eyes than with what I'm looking at. And, of course, that is exactly right.

This shift was first observed (observed, that is, with a proposed explanation for what was being observed) by the Czech physiologist Jan Purkinje in 1819. It's the transition from the rods that control our night vision to the cones that process the bright colours of day. Its oddness has to do with the poised moment between the two.

At the violet transit of that shift I feel as if something peculiar is going on with my brain. For the briefest moment—when the woods on the side of the mountain and the streets of the neighbourhood in which I grew up go black in Hartman's painting—it isn't the walls of our living room or the upholstery of our furniture that brightens. It's the air.

The strange thing about where I grew up (so I told Blake; on that westbound College car after we'd gone to see *It*) was that the pastiche of different styles that is a hallmark of twentieth-century residential architecture meant that almost any horror movie could be accommodated by the neighbourhood. Especially at night. Especially walking home after watching *Dracula's Daughter* and *Night of the Living Dead* at a friend's place. The street lights amid the tree branches gave everything the lighting of *Cat People*.

That's the kind of thing we sometimes talked about. When everything was ordinary. When it was just going to a movie and taking a streetcar home.

13

That fall, Hartman told me that he was spending days in his studio, wrestling with the difficulty of painting the light above my parents' swimming pool. Not, you understand, the reflection of that light on the overhanging leaves and the surrounding brick houses, although that was part of it, but *the light itself*—what the American artist James Turrell calls "the thingness" of light. The light is different above a fifty-by-twenty-five-foot swimming pool. How could it not be?

This is why I'm glad I'm not a painter. Getting the light right would drive me crazy. We can all see that the air above pavement is different from the air above forest. But what makes it different? The air above a brick house is not the same colour as the air above a structure of steel and glass. But what is that colour, exactly? The air above the QEW (the highway that stretches to the horizon of Hartman's painting) can't be unaffected by the presence of all that movement. To see light—to really see it—is a quest of mystic difficulty.

But John Hartman doesn't look much like a visionary. When he works in his studio, which is pretty much every day, he dresses approximately the way a lawyer might dress while on a holiday. He favours khakis and golf shirts and fleecies.

When he breaks from work in his studio and drives over to the L.A. Café in the village of Lafontaine, Ontario, for lunch, he usually has the turkey club sandwich and he'll know pretty much everybody there. He and his wife, Trish, raised their family in Lafontaine. They've lived in their house since 1981—almost the same time that we have lived in ours: the mornings like honey, the evenings like gold, the years turning.

His studio is spacious. It's detached from the house—about the size of a big two-car garage. It's as orderly as a busy, working artist's studio can be.

Hartman is the kind of man who does things properly—things such as building the stretcher for a painting, and cutting the linen, and stapling the turned fabric on the basswood frame so that the surface on which he's going to paint is taut. The glue he uses to seal the linen requires two days of rendering and when it is applied to the stretched surface it can cause the fabric to shrink as much as twenty percent before the glue dries and the fabric returns to its original tension on the frame. This can be tricky. Two-by-four braces need to be screwed in place to stop the wood from twisting. The stress can blow out the mortise and tenon of his precisely squared corners.

The surface of Belgian linen is then spread with titanium white pigment and calcium carbonate ground in linseed oil. Gesso used to be lead-based, and from a purely artistic point of view, white lead is Hartman's preference. But his inclination toward old-fashioned craftsmanship (the glue recipe dates back to the seventeenth century) only goes so far. And so the commercial gesso prepared by D. L. Stevenson is perfectly fine. It's not going to kill him, which is a big plus. It helps prevent the linen from sucking the oil from the pigment and making the paint hard to spread. And it reflects a lustre back through the paint—which, as it happened, was much like what the LSD did. It was like the twinkling of a star. The colours came to us as if at the conclusion of a long journey. This was what light looked like when it first started out.

The various Kings Roads and Lakeside Drives and county lines and small-town, main-street thoroughfares that, if connected in the correct order, became the route between Hamilton and Toronto when my father was young were smoothed into the Queen Elizabeth Way by the time he was a teenager. This was a change of some significance. Were you a landscape artist in the rustic countryside my father remembered between Hamilton and Toronto, you'd notice that the light was different after the highway was built. And just to be clear: it was "*not* named for Elizabeth *the second.*" My father corrected the common misconception with the strained patience of a teacher in a classroom full of dolts. It was a word he liked. "The Queen Elizabeth Way was named for the wife of George VI. Are you some kind of dolt?"

The thingness of that light is in the painting. It informs the horizon. It is the colour of its air. It is different from the light that prevailed during my father's childhood. How could it not be? The highway now carries almost two hundred thousand vehicles daily—more cars than there were people in Hamilton when my father was young. No traffic is visible in Hartman's painting, but that doesn't mean its light isn't. Each of those units of movement glare small, complicated reflections back into the sky. And the light must keep going. Don't you think? What's going to stop its travels through the universe? I picture a distant point in space—a curiously old-fashioned radio antenna—that receives these expanding rings of time. This is the light from my father's boyhood. This is the light (grey above that concrete playground) from mine.

The murder of Donny (slight, dark-haired) along with his sister and his mother, and his father's suicide, did not have the impact that you might expect such a violent event to have on the neighbourhood you can see in the painting. Oh, it was a shock. There are people who were friends and neighbours who are still traumatized by what happened. It came so out of nowhere it was hard to believe. The girls who decided they'd still go to Petula Clark a few days later couldn't believe the seat in their row at O'Keefe Centre was really empty. The minister of the Presbyterian church the family attended had been counselling Donny's father at the time and he told an old friend he was shattered.

But for so spectacular a crime it had no wide reflection. It happened. And then its darkness seemed to close in: no ghost stories, no schoolyard tales continued outward in time. The shadows under Jacob's Ladder consumed themselves, like the black of charred tusks.

Of course, for a while it was the only thing we talked about. Those of us who had never been in Donny's house tried to picture it by bringing the houses we knew to mind. It had a back door. A side window. Basement stairs. It was familiar. We could picture it. And what had they thought the exploding bright second they woke up?

But then, not such a long time later, Donny and his family vanished from our conversation. They were gone.

It was amazing, really. I remember Professor Lindheim reading. A boy falls out of the sky and an expensive delicate ship sails calmly on. Auden. "Musée des Beaux Arts."

I always pointed the house out to anyone I was showing around the neighbourhood. I'm sure I pointed it out to John Hartman when he drove to Hamilton and I took him on my tour. It was just one of several houses I pointed out. Here is the house in which I first heard a Beatles record. Here is the house where, in a rec-room party, I had my first slow dance ("Love is Blue," Paul Mauriat and his Orchestra). And here is where Donny's father killed his whole family. There were five gunshots that night. A dog barked. A few people turned in their sleep. There could have been angels on the old wooden steps and nobody would have noticed.

14

When we were emptying the house after my mother died we came upon snapshots that nobody had seen since forever. These pictures were not remarkable, particularly. There was nothing scandalous or secretive about them. Nor were they old, exactly, although some were not as modern as they once had been. They just hadn't made it into her photograph albums for some reason. They were found at the backs of drawers or tucked away on upper shelves of closets, behind the Levinson's and the Dorsen's shoe-boxes and the long-out-of-fashion tea hats. They'd been put aside for a future filing that never happened.

And what was often the case—not always, but often enough for me to notice—was that those snapshots brought back moments I had not brought to mind—not once—in fifty or sixty years. And yet, there they were. That birthday. That afternoon at the pool.

In much the same way, I would not have been able to say that my childhood had a palette until Hartman painted it. But now that I see it every morning with my coffee, there it is. Had I been asked to name the D. L. Stevenson oil paint colours I would have called them Leather Football Brown and Old Rake-Handle Grey and Oak Tree in Autumn Orange and CCM Bicycle Red and Grass Stain Green. There's a blue with the iron oxide of approaching winter that I'd know anywhere as Underside of Autumn Clouds Over Lake Ontario.

But if you look at the painting closely, as I often do, you will also see colours that are impossible to find amid the chickweed and cocklebur of the Niagara Escarpment. They are too bright to be real. But there they are.

There are greys and pale blues of skin tone in the painting that you'd be hard-pressed to find on my actual face, at least not while I'm alive. There is a blue in the longish, wildish hair that's the colour of a frozen lake. The border between shadow and light across my nose is a dramatically abrupt transition from ruddy cadmium to zinc-white pallor.

The perspective is impossible. Contrary to what the painting suggests, the white threads of waves on Lake Ontario and the distant silhouette of Toronto are not visible from any vantage near my parents' swimming pool. There is no view of grey clouds moving across the late-afternoon sky.

Not that this is a problem. The painting establishes its own weirdly accurate perspective. It is possible to see Toronto from Hamilton, but only from the top of the escarpment and only on a clear day. Even if you could climb high enough into the air above the deep end of the pool to see across the city, the marshlands of Cootes Paradise and the Royal Botanical Gardens wouldn't be in exactly the direction suggested by Hartman's painting. Nor, to the east, can Hamilton's steel mills be seen from the pool's concrete perimeter, or from the diving board, or even from a stepladder. I speak from experience.

In the last years of her life, my mother telephoned from time to time and asked if I wouldn't mind driving in to Hamilton from Toronto to assist her in the ongoing war against invasive vegetation. After my father died in 2011 she lived alone in the house they'd bought in 1952.

My mother didn't like gardeners. They made too much noise. "What's the matter with rakes?" she wanted to know.

As you can see in the painting—from the swirling orange, from the Steinway black, from the cascade of browns and greens and reds—we lived below a wooded hillside. Trees were what you saw from our windows. And trees moving in the breeze were what you heard in my parents' garden. Unless some bloody idiot was using a bloody leaf blower. My mother said.

As measured by sound, Hamilton was a big place. There was the coupling of the freight trains at the TH&B yards. At night the noise, deep and recurrent, seemed as far away as a distant thunderstorm. To the east there were the dim rumblings and the faint humming and the faraway banging and hissing of the Hilton Works and the rod mills. Twenty-four seven, as people say today. Sometimes, depending on the wind, you could hear past all the downtown streets and businesses and lunch counters and offices to the shift siren on the horizon.

Every now and then, though, things did go quiet. Sometimes, strangely so. The painting has the same suspended silence. It's the silence of gliding high over a busy city. Of flying. Something amazing. And it was true. Sometimes in my parents' garden there was just such a silence. It could be only for a moment or two but it was as abrupt as if someone had turned off the sound in a movie.

At random moments in random summer afternoons there were sometimes pauses in the local traffic and the neighbourhood's central air conditioners. By some fluke this pause would coincide with the coffee breaks of the roofers and gardeners who were working nearby. Entirely by accident, every one of dozens of nearby sounds stopped. And this, so my mother maintained, was how things were supposed to be. That's why she never had gardeners. "The racket," she'd say, "would wake the dead."

When my mother first telephoned about the state of the backyard I thought she was more interested in a visit from her eldest child than in actual gardening assistance. In this I was wrong. "You'll need to get the stepladder," she told me as soon as I arrived. "Some of that damned Virginia creeper is high as a house."

The woods of the Niagara Escarpment behind my parents' home are the transition between the Carolinian and the Great Lakes–St. Lawrence forests. My mother was willing to admit that the growing season is shorter in Hamilton than it is in South Carolina. But that didn't mean that she thought its production any less fecund. You couldn't turn your back on it for a second.

Ragwort, goldenrod, walking ferns, tulip trees, Hart's tongue, wild rhubarb, and maple seedlings crept like a guerrilla force from the slopes of the escarpment into our garden during the tropics of a Hamilton summer. To say nothing (so my mother observed as she sat on the grass of the back garden and yanked up the encircling weeds) of the dandelions and thistle and crabgrass.

Only Amelia Street stood between us and the side of the mountain, and it wasn't a very effective barrier against the wilderness. The back lots on the south side of Amelia—on the side that someone from Hamilton would call "under the mountain"—looked more lower-alpine than upper-residential. One back garden had a creek running through it that could get positively torrential in the spring. Amelia was a newer street than Glenfern, one block closer to wild than we were—fitted into the hillside later, it seemed, by developers who knew a good thing when they saw it.

Had it not been for the sewer pipes and wooden hydro poles and property lines that Hamilton's westward growth instigated shortly after the First World War, our property would have remained part of the mixed deciduous tangle of the escarpment. Resisting the garden's inclination to return to its natural state was an ongoing struggle for my mother. "Some of those vines," she said, "would strangle you in your sleep."

Many of the streets near our house—Spruceside, Mapleside, Mountain, Fairmount, Undermount, Ravenscliffe, Hillcrest—had names that attested to the inclining nature of the neighbourhood. There were flooded basements in the spring on our street, and lawnmowers that had to be pushed uphill if they were going to be pushed at all. On more than one occasion my mother may have mentioned: not a single blessed thing in our whole entire house was level.

My mother regarded nature with the wariness of an outpost commander surrounded by enemy forces. And when I got the stepladder from the shed and climbed up on the roof of the pool cabana with the hedge clippers ("before those wild grape vines take over the whole flaming world") there were hornets to be careful about. And there were peach pits and avocado skins and melon rinds that the squirrels had conveyed from the compost. There were glimpses of neighbours' yards, and sometimes even of neighbours. But from the cabana roof there was no view of anything like the one in the painting. There's no view at all. Except of the trees. That's all you saw, really.

15

My father and I played what was still known, in those days, as the Men's. There was a less demanding course. It was nine holes, woven around the Men's back nine. It was known as the Junior Course or, if you were stubbornly old-fashioned, the Ladies'. It was a shade-less, unsurprising par thirty-two. I played it every now and then. Between shifts of my summer job at the steel company, I hitch-hiked out to the golf club a few times a week. So the story that I like to remember telling Blake at our dinner table was not only a story of the one time in my life I played golf with my father. It was the one time in my life I was on the Men's Course. I remember standing up after placing my ball on the first tee and thinking: Whoa, that's a big view. And it was usually around this part of the story that Blake started to laugh.

Colt believed that it was his job to imagine a course that wouldn't completely discourage beginners while, at the same time, would demand a good golfer's best play. He had a genius for this. Which was why the secretary of the Hamilton Golf and Country Club, on behalf of the board of directors, wrote him in the first place.

The course had to be challenging, even infuriating. And yet it had to be a pleasure. Oh, and it had to be beautiful. And if finding the synthesis of these apparent contradictions was not difficult enough, there was another demand made of great golf course designers—an obligation to the very spirit of the game.

It was also Colt's job (Colt felt strongly) to dream of a course on which a truly great player could have a truly great day. If the dream of a perfect round isn't woven into the texture of the course you're on, you're not playing golf. You're practising. Colt believed.

His creative energies were entirely regulated by his knowledge of golf. Golfers, he understood. And golfers, he knew, are nothing if not dreamers. Colt felt that his duty to his clients—part of his duty, anyway—was to accommodate (in landscape) the possibility (in theory) of those rare moments (in time) when the human form (in movement) is aligned with the unfolding universe. Effortless. Free. Imbedded in a course's design had to be the possibility of somebody playing it brilliantly.

"Gentlemen," Colt said to directors gathered round where he stood on the highest point of a burdock-covered hill near the village of Ancaster, a few miles west of the city of Hamilton. This was in the spring of 1914. After a dramatic pause, he raised his voice over the blustery wind. "If you have the money to spend, there is no reason why you should not have one of the finest golf courses in America."

That the Hamilton Golf and Country Club was not in Hamilton, but Ancaster, was only confusing to those who didn't belong to it. Nobody called it the Ancaster club, although for the two or three summers I had a membership, a few older players still called it "the Ancaster course." This was a holdover from the time when it was necessary to distinguish the Ancaster site from the club's original location—which, as it happens, was only a few blocks west of my parents' house on Glenfern. It's a golf course still. Chedoke is owned and operated by the City of Hamilton. Quite a lovely course, actually—possessed of the same incline as our back garden, its fairways lined with the same kinds of trees I'd been able to see from my first bedroom window.

The Chedoke municipal course bracketed the western border of our neighbourhood, merging briefly with the Bruce Trail. The rough of the back nine tumbled westward into sumac and milkweed. It wasn't quite the wilderness out there. But the escarpment was overgrown and tangled enough to pass for wilderness for us. Neighbourhood children were the kind of nuisance the membership of the private club elected to avoid.

By the early years of the twentieth century, the directors could see that the pressure of the city's growth was bound to compromise the pastoral nature of the original course. Westinghouse, Otis Elevator, International Harvester, Procter and Gamble, Dofasco, and Stelco were the foundations of the ambitious city's industry. That was Hamilton's official self-description: the Ambitious City. There was a tobacco company. There was a cotton company. There were wire companies. A friend lived down the street whose grandfather had founded a company that made (only) casket handles. And the presence of this industry gave the city an unfussy practicality. Hamilton was a lunch-bucket town, and it wasn't going to pretend otherwise. There was smog. There was noise. And yes, the harbour was polluted. So what? If you don't want smog, noise, and pollution go to a city that doesn't make steel. That, in broad strokes, was Hamilton's position on environmental protection for the better part of the twentieth century. But this cut both ways for the city's businessmen and lawyers. They weren't sure they wanted to play golf next to a roaring industrial economy.

By the early years of the twentieth century there were complaints about the train tracks across the seventh fairway and about the drifting soot from the TH&B engines that chugged through approach shots. And so the membership of the Hamilton Golf and Country Club paid the celebrated golf course designer Harry Colt to create a private course in Ancaster.

There was some initial concern that the new Hamilton Golf and Country Club was too far away from Hamilton. But those worries passed soon enough. A new affluence was being established by Hamilton's upper middle class, and among its characteristics was the idea that the city of Hamilton, profitable as it was, might not be where you'd want to spend all your time. Resorts flourished. Summer cottages were built. And, as part of the same courtly instinct, country clubs enjoyed their heyday in North America.

The time it took to get from downtown Hamilton to the locker room of the golf club was not a disadvantage. Distance from the bustling corner of King and James became part of the club's cachet. You could get to it from Hamilton by motor car or by the commuter train on the old radial tracks.

Ladies did not wear slacks on the Ancaster course. And certainly not sleeveless sports blouses. If men wore shorts—a relaxation of the dress regulations of which not all members approved—they wore Bermuda shorts, with knee socks.

The golf club was a stately, embassy-like mansion where a buffet was served in the dining room on Sunday evenings. There were

New Year's Eve parties and silver anniversary celebrations and wedding receptions—for members, of course. But it was far from being a social club. Or even, for that matter, a country club. Not really. There was no pool. No tennis courts. There was no croquet or even shuffleboard. It was a golf club—and its chief attraction was the Colt-designed course that spanned outward from its staid, central clubhouse. There was a patio that overlooked the eighteenth green, and its proximity to final putts kept voices down. People were always softly clapping.

Colt was the kind of Englishman for whom plus-fours, tweed jackets and flat caps were created. It was hard to imagine him in anything else. He was already a legendary designer of golf courses by the time the directors of the Hamilton club sought him out. (Formby and Royal Liverpool, Stoke Poges, Swinley Forest, Southfield at Oxford, and Pine Valley in Philadelphia, to name but a few.) The directors wanted Colt's opinion on a property of orchards and pasture just outside of Hamilton. And Colt's opinion, offered that windy May morning in 1914, was encouragingly self-serving.

The directors gathered around him on the hillock he'd chosen for his unhurried survey of the Grange farm near the village of Ancaster. The club's secretary valiantly kept the notes from blowing away. The cuffs of the directors' uniformly grey flannels were by then full of burrs. But this was the great thing about Colt. He paced the land. He breathed it. He felt the terrain in the tread of his burnished Crockett & Jones walking shoes.

The directors followed the Englishman's discerning gaze. And what did they see?

A pig sty.

A cattle slough.

A fence that needed as much attention as the orchard it enclosed.

Muddy tracks around a hill.

This was a nothing kind of place.

"Gentlemen . . ."

Colt's pause was mere convention. He already had everyone's attention.

16

"A touch of polio" must have been what my father said on the Burlington Beach strip when my mother first asked about the thin leg made suddenly obvious by a bathing suit. This would have been on an early date in the late forties. Because that's what my mother always said. "A touch of polio." And it always sounded like she was quoting someone.

A year or two before my father died, we were driving in Hamilton to one of the medical appointments that had become part of his life. He'd been retired for almost fifteen years by then, but he had a doctor's clear, unsentimental view of what his body had in store for him. His thin leg was getting thinner, for one thing. He moved more stiffly than he used to.

He bore the slow approach of decrepitude with some irritation but without surprise. Being a passenger in his own car, being driven to one clinic or another by one of his children or grandchildren was not his idea of fun. But it was inevitable. And anyway, it gave him a chance to remark on Hamilton landmarks, which was something he liked doing.

His knowledge of the city was triggered by the buildings and streets themselves. He was not a collector of books about Hamilton, nor was he a member of any amateur history group. In fact, he sometimes described people who were in his view too obsessively devoted to the preservation of local history as "kooks." But almost any drive anywhere in Hamilton with my father was a chance for him to point out sites and recount ancient gossip. As an example: when we passed the Masonic Temple at the corner of Queen and King Streets he told me about the scandalous circumstances of the death of the man who had built it and whose private residence it had originally been.

Tuckett was the name. Tobacco was the business.

By the end of the nineteenth century the Tucketts had amassed a considerable fortune. It was the kind of wealth that, in the early years of the twentieth century, in Hamilton, was acquired by hard work, a solid, English name, white skin, and the good fortune to catch a small market town transitioning to a sizeable industrial one.

Hamilton had a good port. It was on railway lines. And it was close to the two most important geographic points of reference in the Canadian economy: Toronto and the United States. Now, it was true: if you were poor in Hamilton at the turn of the twentieth century, you could be really poor. Tar-paper-shack poor. Rickets poor. But the thing was: if you were rich, it was possible to get really rich. Black-plumed-carriage rich. Mausoleum rich. It was the kind of money that built the big stone churches that are now mostly empty on Sundays and the mansions that nobody can afford to heat. Some of the money lasted for generations.

For a while, the Tuckett fortune was wealth that could hold its own against the wealth of Pittsburgh or Cleveland or Manchester or Sheffield. As events transpired, it was a fortune that did not endure long, but it was the kind of money that, in more carefully managed Hamilton families, would still be in play a century later. My mother referred to this cluster of mostly related, alma-mater-sharing, golf-playing, summer-cottage-going capitalists as "the fine olds." They were families who had made fortunes in manu-facturing, steel production, cotton, insurance, and tobacco, and part of the pleasure my father took in recounting the story of the Tuckett scandal had to do with the revolutionary tone with which he told it.

The residential locus of Hamilton's wealth shifted westward as the twentieth century unfolded. In general, and true to form, money wanted to get as far away as possible from the chimneys and slag heaps that produced it. As steel production and its atten-dant industries grew, the part of Hamilton that was in the shadow of the mills devolved to rooming houses that smelled of smog out-side and poverty within. Meanwhile, the lawyers and doctors and teachers and accountants and shopkeepers moved steadily away from the open-hearth and rod mills—into more tranquil, tree-lined neighbourhoods. The wealthiest of the businessmen moved further away still, to the country estates of Ancaster and Dundas. There, they actually did shoot skeet and ride to the hounds. Which my father considered a bit much.

Mr. Tuckett's end came suddenly one night but not, alas, in the majestically carved bed he customarily shared with his wife in their grand west-end residence. As we drove past the brick Victorian mansion at the corner of Queen and King Streets that Mr. Tuckett had built my father said, "He died." There was a pause. "In the east end."

And then, as if that were not scandal enough for a prominent Hamiltonian, my father elaborated. "In the arms of his paramour."

My father was proud of where he fit in the order of things. I don't think he'd have put it that way. His pride in anything was usually expressed so quietly you got the sense he preferred nobody to notice. But there was a confidence to his position that was the confidence of his class. His was no stalled ascension. His life was not the acceptance of less than he wished for. This was exactly what he wanted. Wages were earned, savings were made, inheritance was bequeathed, social services were provided. You went to Rotary. You went to art gallery balls. You took up collection on Sundays. And you played golf with your son. Now and then. Before we are all dead and buried. This was the way things were supposed to be.

Seven-thirty a.m. Dr. Macfarlane. Party of two.

Big, I'd have to say. Big was the word that came to mind. And blue. Very, very blue. With white clouds catching the soft magenta of the eastern sky.

Harry Colt's original design at Ancaster—a par seventy-three in those days—was a challenge to the greatest of players while remaining a pleasure (if an exacting one) to the weekend amateur. "Golf," Colt once wrote, "is primarily a pastime and not a penance."

There are more dramatic vistas. And certainly there are more fabled courses. But the view from the first tee at the Hamilton Golf and Country Club—specifically, the view from the first tee on a long-ago August morning—was blue if you looked straight skyward. It was misty in the long golden light of more horizontal observation.

"Crick in your neck?" my father asked. He was not keen on elaborate rituals of loosening up.

And it was the fractal patterns of that light—and not the ordinary objects that reflected it—that held the composition together. The air has its own dazzling. I made a few small adjustments to my grip.

Language and music suggest an order. One word comes before a second word. This note follows that. What we normally understand as the sequential nature of time is as predictable as a golf course. The dogleg of the eighth always comes after the footbridge of the seventh. The putter follows the nine iron which follows the three which follows the driver.

The Hamilton course was delightful, even for non-golfers. It was not uncommon in the club's early days for non-players to accompany a foursome just for the pleasure of the walk.

I made the first feathery strokes of the head of my driver as if to make sure that no adjustment had been made to its weight or length since the last time I'd picked it up.

In front of a right-hander's stance, and in receding order, there was the pro shop and the putting green and the driving range and, beyond the line of oak that marked the edge of the club's property, the village of Ancaster's water tower. It was a pleasant view—notable, at seven-thirty in the morning, for the absence of any human form and humble in everything except the generosity of proportion. No part of it was in any way spectacular. And yet everything was exactly as you'd wish it to be. And it was that view, I think, that saved me. This is going to be beautiful, I realized—meaning not my play. That remained to be seen. What I meant was: we were stepping into a landscape that had been designed to be, among other things, beautiful. The light, you'd have to say, was perfect. I mean: perfect.

Were you starting to turn your attention to the business of striking a very small white ball with the accelerating curve of your drive it was hard to imagine a better place to be or a better time of day to be there. It was a calming view. Which was a good thing. Calm was what I was looking for in my swing. To be calm was my objective.

The technique that J. Douglas Edgar championed could not be broken down into mechanics. It could not be reduced to a series of stills. What Edgar called *the movement* was a continuum of adjustment, and to teach it Edgar created a wooden gate that bracketed the practice tee. A player's first objective, in Edgar's view, was not to hit the ball. The goal was to swing a club in such a way that its head passed through the gate. Hitting the ball would automatically happen—with *the movement.* It was the fluidity of the stroke that was the secret of its success. Edgar called this fluidity "abandonment." He said that golfers had to let "a little joie de vivre creep in." He wasn't fastidious about where the backswing began and where the follow-through ended, but he was insistent that a stroke's central four feet—the two feet before contact with the ball and the two feet after—be approached by a player with mindful focus. The ball, he said, was merely an incident in a swing. *"Meditation and concentration are the way to a life of serenity." —Baba Ram Dass.* Greetings from Barstow, California.

17

Blake loved to dance, which is something I never really saw him do. I'd seen him on dance floors at weddings and anniversary parties. But I'd never seen him really dance—dance, as in what he was going to do when he got better. Late at night. With friends. In a club I'd never heard of, happily lost in the big techno kerthwump of music I didn't know.

So this is something I imagined, not saw. But now that I think of it, I realize that I imagined it a lot during the four and a half years of his illness: Blake free of all those lines and tubes and wires. I pictured him with his arms raised, turning round and round in the swirling lights of a dance floor somewhere.

He hated being attached to monitors and IV units. There were long stretches in the hospital and at home when there were several at once. And when, from time to time, he was cut loose (when he was in remission or headed that way), Blake and I sometimes celebrated his freedom by going out to Harbord or College to get something to eat. And if I may. Another word of advice: if your son or daughter asks if you want to grab a bite, say yes. By then, just walking down a sidewalk—just moving freely through the air— was a pleasure Blake did not take for granted. He said that sometimes in the hospital he thought about running, or riding a bike, or dancing. I was amazed that he was as patient and as careful with the PICC lines and IV units as he was. But by the end of his life his patience was gone.

The flies he kept trying to whisk away from his face weren't flies at all, but hungry, pecking birds. Ravens. The tubes he kept trying to pull away from his arms, from his legs, from his chest stayed attached because his mother's hands took his and folded them in hers. She guided his hands back gently to the hospital sheets.

"Hush," she said.

He had her long fingers. You saw that immediately when they were together. She soothed him as best she could. It was not clear that he heard her.

A nurse, still as a stone, stands to one side of the bed. She is attending to all this. The nurse's posture is excellent, her handsome face solemn. Her presence is calming.

Children fall from the sky. Young soldiers die. Refugees drown. The nurse knows how all those mothers feel. This is her gift. Her beautiful eyes gleam with all the sadness in the world.

Hush, she is saying.

Hush.

Of all the rooms in our house in Toronto, the dining room has changed the least over the years. It's been the way it is now since the kids were little.

Although the fabric on the chairs is over twenty years old, it looks perfectly fine. We are approaching the third decade of Janice wanting to change the light over the dinner table. Whether it was just the four of us, or whether we were joined by friends and family, it's the same as it always was. If I want to picture Blake, the dining room is a good place to do it. Take as an example: that long-ago dinner conversation when apropos of "Lucy in the Sky with Diamonds," a friend of ours (Blake's godfather as I recall) brought up the eighteen holes I once played with my father.

"Yes," Blake said, turning toward me with renewed interest. "What about that time you played golf with Granddad?"

Harry Colt's courses were celebrated for their embrace of landscape. He had strong views on these things. He once wrote: "Too much stress cannot be laid upon the necessity of seeing and using the natural features present on each course to the fullest extent."

I was anxious during the drive with my father to the golf club. That was putting it mildly. I could see that things could go very badly. This was a possibility that had to be admitted.

I was sitting in the passenger seat in madras Bermuda shorts, beige knee socks, and navy-blue golf shirt. The window was open, and my right arm was crooked into the rush of air, as per usual in the summer in our car. No options.

It wasn't obvious that the effects of the LSD were diminishing. In fact, I wasn't absolutely certain they weren't still increasing.

This left the possibility that a golf course, or a golf club, or a golf ball would present a challenge beyond my capacities. And if that happened, I could not see what would happen next. Would I have to say to my father: I can't do this?

We were approaching the clubhouse. It was a little after seven. I'd been doing my best to go over what I could remember of my golf lessons. That seemed a better option than panic. And while this proved to be more effective than I could have reasonably expected it to be, it wasn't what saved me. What saved me was: That winding creek. That gentle copse. Those distant, cloud-shadowed slopes of lime green and cinnabar.

My father intended to walk the course. He always did. He viewed electric golf carts with the same distrust as power mowers. He pulled a handcart, but I chose to shoulder my bag. I wasn't sure about operating a handcart under the circumstances. And the circumstances were (so I made sure everyone at the dinner table understood): killer windowpane. The morning fell through the trees in golden shafts that a Hollywood cinematographer might have thought too picturesque.

Anxiety precedes even social rounds of golf, and that anxiety, as J. Douglas Edgar wrote in his unorthodox 1920 guidebook, *The Gate to Golf*, has an obvious source. "Years ago I began to wonder how it was that some players had so much difficulty in playing to a certain average standard, and I thought it must be due to a fear of something, that something must be worrying them, and gradually I came to the conclusion that it was the ball that worried and beat them."

I took my time. I gave my mechanics a good deal of thought before I took my one practice swing. My father rarely commented on such things, but he somehow communicated that he took a dim view of multiple practice swings.

My father wasn't a fast player. Nor was he slow. He had a steady, direct pace, and if his shots were never spectacular, they were rarely disastrous. He played, more or less, as he expected to play. His approach to a green was an articulated zigzag—as if he were taking precaution against enemy fire. He avoided triumph with the same choppy but consistent stroke by which he avoided calamity.

He did not actually voice his concerns until we'd played the sixth. It was a narrow, upward-sloping par three, with a central network of sand traps that I initially took to be rivulets of lava.

Either you tried to go over them off the tee (an attempt fraught with peril on three sides of the green) or you went short and unspectacular, settling for a not-all-that-easy uphill lie into a backdrop of trees and underbrush.

"Tough luck," my father said when my soaring five iron dead-stopped in the left S-turn of sand, about thirty feet short of the hole-in-one I had in mind. He'd taken it easy himself, and was lying nicely in front of the sand to the right. He pitched up, over one of the hillocks that guarded the green. These arms of elevation looked, in approach, like the banks of an ancient river, long dry. It was an effect that Colt found pleasing.

It wasn't my play that alarmed my father. Because, in fact, I played pretty well. (For me, I mean. Let's not get carried away.) And the reason I was playing pretty well was because my review in the car of anything I could remember the golf pro telling me came as something of a revelation. LSD will do that.

I had not previously understood how a golf swing worked. It was as simple as that. I could never remember the components of a stroke in sequence because (it was starting to dawn on me as I took my first practice swing that morning) they are not executed in sequence. They happen all at once. There are adjustments for things that have not yet occurred. There are conclusions to what has not begun. The elements of a good swing coalesce into the single, fluid motion that J. Douglas Edgar called *the movement,* and when that happens the club head drives cleanly through the gateway of golf.

No, I was hitting the ball just fine. Much better than usual, at any rate. The only problem (so my father was beginning to notice) was that I could not keep score. Absolutely could not. Totally, could not. "Oh, come on," my father said the first time it happened. This was on the first green. "You must remember what you just did."

On the sixth, my father pulled his scorecard from the back pocket of his light-blue slacks—as he had for the fifth, fourth, third, second, and first. He asked, just as he had previously asked, "What did you shoot?" And for the sixth time that morning I had no idea. Not a clue.

The pencil stayed poised.

"Are you all right?" he asked, not unkindly.

No matter how resolutely I set out to remember the events of each hole, I didn't. There was always too much that happened—too many unexpected connections, too many unanticipated associations, too many things that made me laugh, and way too much beauty. What happened on the third? What happened on the seventeenth? I had no idea. I couldn't keep them straight. Some holes were instantaneous. Some were eternities. Some changed entirely partway through. I kept losing track of the line between putting out to end a hole and driving to begin the next. And there was so much going on—that monarch butterfly, that moss in that stream, that cloud—I was constantly diverted from my stroke tally. In fact, I was beginning to find the very idea of keeping score quite funny. Which didn't help. I could never work my way back through the intricacies of the recent past.

After the sixth, my father marked my progress from stroke to stroke from wherever on the fairway (or in the rough or on a green) he was standing when I completed a shot. "That's three," he called. "That's four." It was the longest conversation we ever had.

At one point I said, "Stop it. You're making me laugh." To which he answered—accurately—that laughing didn't seem to be doing my game any harm. And it was true. I'd been laughing quite a lot, all the way around our eighteen holes. I won thirty cents that day.

I'll bet that we didn't hug when we got home. We probably shook hands. I would have thanked him for the game.

Blake's counts were tanking that December. Sometimes he couldn't lie down. Sometimes, he couldn't sit, couldn't walk. Sometimes he was in such pain I thought my heart would break with helplessness. But sometimes hugging worked. Sometimes—occasionally in the middle of the night—we'd stand together beside his bed in the apartment in the basement of our house, in the room directly below the living room—and I'd hold him, my twenty-nine-year-old son, sometimes for as long as half an hour. Me: hair grey. Him: thin as the young Bob Dylan, and pale, and handsome as can be. And that's how I know that as a young man his hair smelled exactly as it had when he was a little boy. He caught a rubber ball almost twenty times in a row in the dappled sunlight of my parents' back garden and I lifted him triumphantly. You couldn't see the water of the pool from where we were. But it was there. I didn't think that light would ever change.

There are a lot of things that can go wrong with a golf stroke. But for some reason, on the summer morning I played with my father, they didn't. My shoulders were squared over my grip. The crack of my driver felt clean as a whistle, but as the ball shot into the blank blue sky it was, for that second, out of my line of vision.

My eyes were where the pro had told me to keep them: on the vibrating but otherwise untouched tee.

"Not bad," my father said.

His drive rolled a little short and just to the left of mine. "Beautiful morning," he said. "What do you say to ten cents a hole?"

This was a good start.

afterword

And all of a sudden, the painting is gone.

Well, not exactly all of a sudden—not if you are thinking in terms of the planning that goes into an exhibition at an art gallery.

Superframe had been in touch. Superframe is the art handling service contracted by the McMichael and Woodstock art galleries. This is where the painting is going—to the McMichael Canadian Art Collection in Kleinburg, about a half-hour drive to the northwest of downtown Toronto. It will be part of an exhibition called *John Hartman: Many Lives Mark This Place*—twenty-eight large portraits and nine smaller studies, all writers, all portrayed in landscapes or cityscapes important to them. After the McMichael the exhibit will tour to six other Canadian galleries, including Canada House, in Trafalgar Square. This show has been in the works for many months. Superframe emailed to say the team would be at our house at three o'clock on a Monday in late February.

The two young men who showed up were unimpeded by all the monitor cables and patch cords on the living-room floor. A few microphone stands had to be moved. It took them about twenty minutes to crate and wrap the painting. And then, just like that, the big, unframed rectangle of stretched Belgian linen was gone.

So it wasn't as if I didn't know what was going to happen. It wasn't as if we weren't given all kinds of warning. It was just that when it did (actually happen) I wasn't expecting so much to vanish.

But this is what happens when you live with a painting. It has a particular energy. It has a presence in a room that is more active than a poster or reproduction, and when that presence is gone it's gone completely. Call it a vibe if you want because that's sort of what it is. It's something that's hard to put your finger on, but when it's not there, it's really not there. It was like when my father died. The same with Blake.

I don't remember much about my father's funeral—except that we sang "Show Me the Way to Go Home." Not counting hymns, it was the only thing we'd ever heard him sing. And the only time he ever sang it was when he was driving us back from Christmas dinners at our relatives in Burlington and Dundas. I must have been ten years old before I realized the song wasn't specifically about being tired and sleepy and wanting to get home to bed in Hamilton.

Blake wore a tartan sports jacket to his grandfather's funeral. The jacket had originally been his great-grandfather's. It had been altered, probably in the late 1940s, to fit my father when he had been as young and slender as Blake. When my father was in his early seventies, he decided that he'd grown too heavy to wear it and he gave it to me—although I wasn't getting any smaller either, at that stage of my middle age.

It fit me, just, but it did not compliment my figure—which, aside from pockets, is all I really ask of a jacket. It hung in my closet unworn for years. It was, I felt, almost comically square. But what did I know? The wheels of fashion turn. Blake, who had an eye for these things, decided to wear it to his grandfather's funeral. This was a sign of respect and affection. But he was also guided by the same instinct that had served him so well in vintage clothing stores from the time he was a teenager. I remember being surprised by how cool a jacket from a long-gone Hamilton haberdashery looked on our handsome twenty-year-old son.

Otherwise, my father's funeral is a blur. But what I do recall clearly about that day is driving back to Glenfern from Melrose United Church after the service. Our route was along the same grid of streets that I imagine I can see in the Hartman painting. My mother was silent beside me.

The verandas and the front walks and the trees we were passing were having the effect that the west end of Hamilton often has on me. It seems to be an automatic response. I can't be on those sidewalks without feeling the approach of another phase of time. I start to imagine that perhaps, if I remember enough, I will find myself back in that light. Every detail of remembrance will sparkle with reality. This is what John Hartman calls the imaginary space. Over which we have no control. Greetings from Route 66. Be here. Now.

And it could be a windowpane, I suppose: looking out to that particularly bare light. It always seemed to be a cloudless, cold Sunday morning when we drove Granny to church. I remember that with the weirdest clarity. Sometimes we drove her to our house after the service. "I'd practically have a nervous breakdown," my mother used to say whenever the subject of entertaining her mother-in-law came up.

Driving the same route after my father's funeral, my mother expressionless beside me, her attention somewhere straight ahead, I was thinking about how my memory operates. I can't remember a password to save my life. I'm hopeless with birthdays, including my own. But if presented with an embarkation point (a neighbourhood, for one example; a painting, for another) my memory can be quite detailed. So I found. As we drove home from Melrose that day. After we thanked my parents' old friends—the old friends who were left, that is—for coming to the funeral. And that's what I'm talking about. Because I could see them all: up at the pool, laughing in the cabana. I could see all those old friends when they were young. Long ago. In that light. I could see details down to the crabmeat spread and the plastic highball glasses. And, as always, I ended up wondering where that light is. It was so real, for so long. It can't just be gone.

Heading along Homewood Avenue, turning onto Kent, I had the feeling that if I wasn't driving a car, if I were in the passenger seat and could turn my unrushed gaze from one side of the street to the other, I would know every curb of sidewalk and storm sewer and privet hedge. This is hardly surprising. I walked those streets, ran them, biked them, played catch and ball hockey on them, delivered newspapers, went to church and back on them, and was driven along them over and over. I was under the umbrella of trees in Hartman's painting thousands of times.

On my evening walks through my old neighbourhood, memories sometimes came as thickly as Hartman's knife-fulls of D.L. Stevenson oils. One beside the other. No space between. Even so, it was always understood (at least, by me it always was) that my Hamilton had nothing like the texture and depth and rich idiosyncrasy of my father's. That's what I told Caroline and Blake when they were little and they asked questions about where I grew up. I'd tell them about playing on the side of the mountain. And I'd tell them what the garden was like before the pool. But reaching further into the past I'd get a little hazy. Oh, I said to them. We should ask Grandad.

On our way back from his funeral, as we turned from Kent onto Aberdeen, I was thinking how many more layers of history he

knew of these streets than I do. How many more names of however many more former owners of however many addresses. How
many more stories and characters and ghosts of old neighbourhood rumour. How many more long-departed. I was thinking
about how densely populated his imaginary space of Hamilton
was. We were turning onto Spruceside Avenue at the time. And
that's when I realized that my father's world was gone.

"You're making me sound like a rube," I can easily imagine
him saying. And, yes, he knew bigger cities than Hamilton. He'd
lived in Toronto and New York. He knew his way around London
and Paris. But really, the streets of Hamilton, Ontario, Canada—
the red brick houses and hedges and sidewalks that we were
driving past—were the grid of the one place in the world he knew
really, really well. His history of Hamilton was so deeply inside
him it was part of who he was. Evidently. It was gone when he
was gone.

The two young guys from Superframe were only slightly inconvenienced by the Deluxe Reverb-Amps and the Roland and
Yamaha keyboards. There's a big Kendrick tweed. It's the biggest
amplifier in the band, actually—our harmonica player's. There's a
third electric organ leaning against the wall, and I was with Blake
when he chose the red Mapex drum kit. I remember that we had to
convince each other that we didn't like it best just because it looked
so cool. There are currently (I just counted) six electric guitars in
the living room, and it's not a very wide room to begin with. But
these were obstacles that presented no difficulty to Superframe.
They'd seen worse.

In no time at all, really, the painting was down. Just as quickly
it was wrapped, signed-for, and loaded into the temperature-
controlled truck. That was to be expected. It was the empty wall
that took me by surprise.

William Blakely Macfarlane 1988-2018

those Blake would have thanked

The nurses, doctors, and staff of Princess Margaret, Toronto General, Toronto Western, and Mount Sinai Hospitals

Friends: Cheryl Atkinson and Don Schmitt, Bruce Bailey, Sam Bailey, Karen and Tom Bell, Cathrin Bradbury, Laura Bradbury, Jessica Bradley and Geoffrey James, Kevin Breit, Shauna Cairns Gundy, George Cohon, Tecca Crosby, Mona Cui and Weixian Min, Lorna Day and David Wilson, Charlotte Day Wilson, Diana and Nigel Dickson, Ann Dowsett Johnston, Leslie Fischook and David Wallen, Alyssa Gerber, Joanna and Meric Gertler, Isabel Gertler, Miles Gertler, Libby and Hope Gibson, Alison Gordon, Gillian and Ron Graham, Mimi Graham, James Graham, Lorraine Greey, Ali Greey, Meredith Greey, Susan Grimbly and Ian Pearson, Lily Harmer and Douglas Cameron, Deborah Hope, Paddy Horrigan, Julia Hune-Brown, Roz Ivey, Charles James, Roz Kavander, Dave Kazala, Lisa Kent and Danny Greenspoon, Daisy Kling, Al Kling, Sari Lightman, Romy Lightman, Hereward Longley, John Macfarlane, Pat MacKay, Alexandra Mackenzie, Ryan Mandelbaum, Janice McAuley, Murray McLauchlan, Marybeth McTeague and David Hayes, Sarah and Tom Milroy, Effy Min, Corey Moranis, Vanessa Nicholas, Nathalie and Sean O'Connor, Maria Pasquino and Richard Longley, Nine Pos, Bob Rae, Lynda Reeves, Liz Rykert and John Sewell, Deborah Scheuneman and Vezi Tayeb, Johanna Schneller and Ian Brown, Cornelia Schuh and Michiel Horn, Scout, Adam See, Myra and George See, Gail Singer, Linda Sully, Diane Walker, Michèle White, Bonnie Whitehall and Judd Brucke, Ellen Vanstone, Simmy and Mark Zaret

Family

DAVID MACFARLANE was born in Hamilton. His family memoir, *The Danger Tree*, was described by Christopher Hitchens as "one of the finest and most intriguing miniature elegies that I have read in many a year." Macfarlane's novel *Summer Gone* was short-listed for the Giller Prize. Based on *The Danger Tree*, *The Door You Came In*, a two-man show (co-written and performed with Douglas Cameron), has been produced to acclaim from St. John's, Newfoundland, to Stratford, Ontario. Macfarlane lives in Toronto with his wife, the designer Janice Lindsay.

A NOTE ABOUT THE TYPE

The body of *Likeness* has been set in Filosofia, a typeface designed in 1996 by Zuzana Licko, co-founder of Émigré Fonts. The face is a modern interpretation of the classic Bodoni, allowing for applications that Bodoni's extreme contrasts cannot address, namely good readability in smaller text sizes.